# Kebabs

# DEDICATION

For Zoey

Brimming with creative inspiration, how-to projects, and useful information to enrich your everyday life, Quarto Knows is a favorite destination for those pursuing their interests and passions. Visit our site and dig deeper with our books into your area of interest: Quarto Creates, Quarto Cooks, Quarto Homes, Quarto Lives, Quarto Drives, Quarto Explores, Quarto Gifts, or Quarto Kids.

© 2017 Quarto Publishing Group USA Inc.
Text © 2017 Derrick Riches and Sabrina Baksh

First published in the United States of America in 2017 by
The Harvard Common Press, an imprint of
Quarto Publishing Group USA Inc.
100 Cummings Center
Suite 265-D
Beverly, Massachusetts 01915-6101
Telephone: (978) 282-9590
Fax: (978) 283-2742
QuartoKnows.com
Visit our blogs at QuartoKnows.com

All rights reserved. No part of this book may be reproduced or utilized, in any form or by any means, electronic or mechanical, without prior permission in writing from the publisher. All images in this book have been reproduced with the knowledge and prior consent of the artists concerned, and no responsibility is accepted by producer, publisher, or printer for any infringement of copyright or otherwise, arising from the contents of this publication. Every effort has been made to trace the copyright holders and ensure that credits accurately comply with information supplied. We apologize for any inaccuracies that may have occurred and will resolve inaccurate or missing information in a subsequent reprinting of the book.

Harvard Common Press titles are also available at discount for retail, wholesale, promotional, and bulk purchase. For details, contact the Special Sales Manager by email at specialsales@quarto.com or by mail at The Quarto Group, Attn: Special Sales Manager, 100 Cummings Center, Suite 265-D, Beverly, MA 01915, USA.

21 20 19 18 17     1 2 3 4 5

ISBN: 978-1-63159-906-4

Digital edition published in 2017

Library of Congress Cataloging-in-Publication Data available.

Design: Elizabeth Van Itallie
Page Layout: *tabula rasa* graphic design
Photography: Michael Piazza Photography
Photo Stylist: Sally Staub

Printed in China

75 Spectacular
Recipes for
Grilling

# Kebabs

Derrick Riches
and
Sabrina Baksh

HARVARD
COMMON
PRESS

# Contents

6   Introduction: Skewers and Fire

18   CHAPTER 1: BEEF KEBABS
42   CHAPTER 2: PORK AND LAMB KEBABS
74   CHAPTER 3: CHICKEN AND TURKEY KEBABS
98   CHAPTER 4: FISH AND SEAFOOD KEBABS
116   CHAPTER 5: VEGETABLE AND FRUIT KEBABS

138   About the Authors
139   Acknowledgments
140   Index

# INTRODUCTION
# Skewers and Fire

At the beginning of just about every grilling cookbook is a short little story about how humans first learned to make fire, how they then discovered they could cook food over the fire, and how what we call grilling today is a direct descendant of these ancient discoveries. It's an excellent story. Fire is great. What the stories usually leave out is the first cooking utensil our ancestors used: the stick. The stick holds the food out of the fire. It allows for temperature control, easy handling, finesse, and the artistry of the chef. The stick, or as we shall now refer to it, the skewer, gives us the kebab, and kebabs are the perfect food.

The kebab is truly the universal dish. Every culture has some variation of it, and they can be found in the fanciest restaurants or served hot from a street corner food cart. As a meal, snack, appetizer, dessert, or side dish, the kebab is as versatile as pizza and as numerous as the hamburger. From minced meat seekh kebabs to pork souvlaki to steak and peppers, this one dish has it all—except the respect it deserves.

Thread meat, vegetables, fruit, or virtually any type of food onto a skewer, throw it over an open flame, and you will be eating within minutes. The kebab is a brilliant concept but unfortunately overlooked as most people have simply not taken the time to explore all of the possibilities. In this book, the old patio kebab composed of overcooked vegetables and tough, dried out meat is replaced with tender, flavorful, and simple-to-prepare dishes. It is our goal to reintroduce this concept with both global and familiar fare, leading you, the reader, to explore the world of kebabs.

# The Secrets of the Perfect Kebab

With all the possibilities that the kebab offers, there are a few secrets to perfection. What must be avoided is a dry kebab with burnt food or one that is overcooked on one end and raw on the other. As with all grilling, knowing the fire, proper placement, turning, and timing are the keys to success. But don't worry. Kebabs are easy. Just follow three basic rules:

**1.** Don't over pack! Trying to force too much food on a skewer will cause it to cook slowly and unevenly. Loosely thread the skewer so that heat can move about the food evenly. Generally, a kebab cooks faster on the ends than it does in the center. Leaving a little space between the foods in the middle will solve this problem.

**2.** Cut foods to the proper size. Giant cubes of meat will take longer to cook through. This will result in a burnt exterior and a raw center. The meat used for kebabs should be cut into approximately 1- to 1½-inch (2.5 to 4 cm) cubes. Getting each piece cut to approximately the same size results in a better kebab.

**3.** Mix meats and vegetables that belong together. In the 1950s and 60s, when people dressed formally for cookouts and drank martinis, there was a bad habit of mixing the wrong vegetables on the skewer. Pearl onions, cherry tomatoes, and canned mushrooms do not belong together on a skewer. Use thin squares of onions or bell peppers, thick cuts of squash, and fresh mushrooms. Since most vegetables are prone to sliding off of the skewer, always start and end with a good piece of meat or a heartier vegetable.

# Types of Skewers

Using the right skewer for the job is one of the most important decisions you can make. Hey, you bought a book on kebabs, so you should also invest in the right kind of skewers. In fact, you should probably have a few different kinds on hand to tackle all the recipes here.

**BAMBOO SKEWERS:** Kebabs are the world's most popular street foods and for the person selling them from a cart, a cheap and disposable skewer is vital. Unfortunately, people use bamboo skewers far too frequently. While these are great for thin strips of meat, as you would use for Yakitori, or for quickly grilling items like fruits or some vegetables, they are not ideal for thick cuts of meat. Bamboo simply won't do for minced meat kebabs like koftas and seekh kebabs. Yes, as some authorities will advise, bamboo skewers can be soaked for 15 to 30 minutes in water to help prevent them from burning, but this will only buy 30 seconds to one minute of grilling time before they are reduced to ashes on the ends. If bamboo is the only way to go, lay strips of aluminum foil on the grill so that the exposed ends are protected from the fire while the food meets the cooking grate.

**METAL SKEWERS:** There is a great selection that is easy to find and infinitely reusable, but make sure to avoid cheap metal skewers. Look for

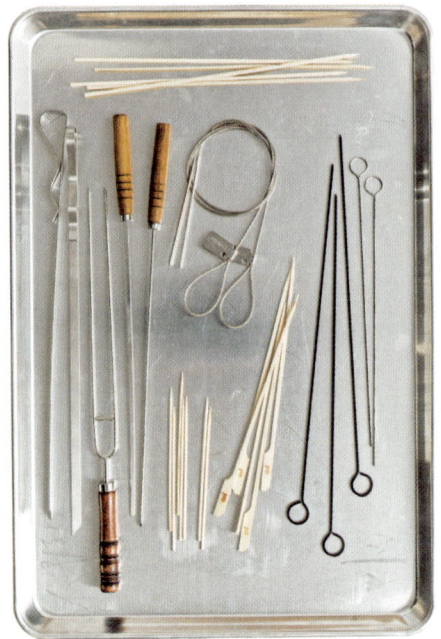

stainless steel skewers with a flat blade shape. Round skewers don't hold food as well and make it impossible to turn the kebab effectively (the skewer turns, but the food doesn't). The skewers should be ¼ inch (6 mm) in diameter so that they will securely grip the food and can be flipped easily.

**SWORD SKEWERS:** These large stainless steel skewers have a ½-inch (1.5 cm) wide blade that can be up to two feet (0.5 m) in length and are frequently found in Middle Eastern and South Asian food stores. These big skewers are necessary for the traditional koftas and seekh kebabs as well as larger cuts of meat and vegetables. A set of these will really impress your guests.

**FLEXIBLE SKEWERS:** A few years back, a company named Fire Wire set out to improve the skewer. Their reinvention resulted in a steel cable device with a point on one end and a loop on the other. Foods are threaded on, just like any other skewer, but since the steel cable is flexible, the pointed end can be bent around and hooked through the loop. This makes for a versatile skewer that is perfect for all manner of traditional kebabs. We like these skewers because with a heat-resistant glove, the pointed end can be held and the whole kebab flipped in one easy motion. The bend in the cable holds everything in place. Also, the skewers can be turned and manipulated into any shape necessary. These are perfect for use on small or round grills.

# Rubs, Marinades, Bastes, and Brines

**RUBS:** The secret to turning plain chunks of meat and simple vegetables into a spectacular meal is in the flavorings. Rubs are simply a collection of salt, herbs, and spices that are applied before grilling. They are a method of combining flavors in a way that balances the outcome and are so much more than just a random sprinkling of seasonings. By adding a spice rub 30 minutes ahead of time, the flavors will properly combine and have a chance to seep into the surface of the food.

**MARINADES:** Lean cuts of meat dry out quickly when exposed to intense heat and tend to lack flavor. A good marinade will add moisture, flavor, and the fats necessary to compensate for this. Yes, it is true that marinades only help a little with tenderization, but these are vital to dishes like Yakitori, souvlaki, and Greek-style lamb kebabs. A good marinade coats the food in flavor.

**BASTES:** On top of the grill is the perfect place to build flavors, and this is best achieved with a baste. A good basting sauce should be thin, but flavorful. Several applications of a basting sauce will really season the kebabs. For this reason, investing in a good basting brush is a must. Note that bastes that contain sugar can cause the kebab to burn (sugar burns at 265°F [129°C]), so make sure to keep a close eye on those.

**BRINES:** A brine is a magical solution and for the small pieces of meat that generally find their way onto kebabs, it is also a quick and easy way to make something spectacular. Some cuts of meat, though lean and flavorful, need help to retain moisture. Brining is the best way to make a good cut of meat better. Pork and poultry in particular benefit from a good brining. The method is straightforward. A brine is simply a salt water solution that meats are soaked in for an allotted amount of time. There must be enough brine to completely cover the meat or poultry, but for kebabs, that is usually no more than a few cups (700 to 950 ml). A proper brine is 1 part salt to make it a brine, 1 part sugar to balance the flavor, and 16 parts water. Combine vigorously to ensure that the salt and sugar are completely dissolved. Place the brine and the meat in a nonmetal container (metal can react with the salt) and refrigerate for 30 minutes to an hour. For small amounts of meat, a good quality resealable plastic bag works well for brining, but any plastic or glass bowl, covered, will work just as well.

If a meat has been brined, it will contain all the salt it needs for flavor. **When brining, omit the salt from spice and bastes**; otherwise, the salt content may be too high to be palatable in the finished recipe.

## Basic Brine Recipe

MAKES 2 CUPS (475 ML) BRINE

- 2 tablespoons (36 g) table salt or 3 tablespoons (25 g) kosher salt
- 2 tablespoons (26 g) white sugar
- 2 cups (475 ml) cold water

Combine all the ingredients and stir until the salt and sugar are completely dissolved. Pour into a large resealable bag along with up to two pounds (900 g) of cubed meat. Allow to brine for 30 minutes to 1 hour. Do not brine for more than 2 hours. At the end of the brining time, pour the entire contents into a colander and lightly rinse to remove any excess surface salt. Toss to remove as much liquid as possible and pat the meat dry with paper towels before threading on the kebabs.

# Vegan and Vegetarian Substitutions

The kebab is the best method for grilling vegetarian or vegan options. The blending of small pieces of vegetables with meat alternatives like tofu or seitan is perfect for a cooking method generally associated with large cuts of meat. Most of the recipes in this book can be easily altered to a vegetarian or vegan dish by simply replacing the cubed meat items with equally sized pieces of tofu, seitan, tempeh, firm cheeses like halloumi or kasseri, or additional vegetables. The seasonings, marinades, and bastes will work just as well with these substitutions. Just be sure to adjust the marinating times by half.

When using tofu, look for the firmest you can find. Extra firm is the best option. The biggest problem with using tofu on skewers is that the stick can easily cut through it. Gentle handling and a well-oiled cooking grate will alleviate most of this problem. Using vegetables to help space and hold the tofu pieces in place will also help.

Mushrooms also make a fantastic alternative, particularly with beef kebabs. Hearty mushrooms like Cremini or Portobello are the best choice. They hold up to the grill, are readily available, and can be cut to the proper size and shape to make the best vegetarian kebabs.

Unfortunately, none of these options work well for a minced meat substitution, particularly on the grill. Seitan and tempeh are far from malleable and tofu is too soft. While most vegetarians and vegans rely on various vegetable, bean, legume, and grains like quinoa to replicate meatballs and koftas, these are best baked in the oven or fried in skillets. Attempting to grill these items, even on the most well-oiled grill grates, will produce undesired results. They will break apart very easily or simply fall off of the skewers before they even have a chance to hit the grill. These few minced meat recipes pose the only restriction to vegan and vegetarian diets.

# How to Thread a Kebab

The meat that goes on a kebab is generally divided into three types: cubes, strips, and minced or ground meat. There are different reasons for each that have to do with tradition, tenderness, and speed of cooking. For a kebab to cook evenly, it is important that all its parts be cut as consistently as possible. Each individual piece should be as uniform as possible. Mixing large chunks with smaller cubes will lead to a mixture of under- and overcooked pieces and that must be avoided to make the perfect kebab. Each recipe in this book will tell you how to cut all the pieces that fit onto the skewer for maximum success.

**CUBES:** For more tender cuts of meat and kebabs that are going to include vegetables, the cube is the best solution. Cubes of meat should be 1 to 1¼ inches (2.5 to 3 cm) on each side. Of course, the natural shape and structure of a cut of meat doesn't always make this an easy proposition, but uniformity is the key here. If a suitable cut of meat can't be found in the grocery store's cases, talk to the butcher. For many of the recipes here, asking the butcher for a 1 inch (2.5 cm) thick cut is the easiest solution. Packages of precut "kebab" meat, stew meat, or other such items are seldom the best solution. These are usually leftover pieces from some other cut and should be avoided as much as possible. Do your own cutting and you will get a much better kebab. In general, roasts are the best selection for making kebabs since they have the thickness necessary and are generally less expensive.

When threading cubes of meat onto skewers, go through the flat side of the cube and out the opposite side. To get the maximum effect of the searing capabilities of hot cooking grates, we want the cube of meat to sit flat. A perfect kebab made from cubes of meat should have four even sides and each of these sides should spend at least a minute or two on the cooking surface. This reduces the cooking time and improves the surface texture of the meat. When making these types of kebabs with interspaced vegetables, the vegetable pieces should match the size of the meat to prevent them from lifting the meat off the cooking surface.

To ensure proper cooking, cubes of meat should be temperature checked with a reliable and fast-reading meat thermometer. Test the temperature toward the center of the meat, but avoid getting too close to the skewer. Metal skewers, in particular, will be considerably hotter than the meat itself and, for the sake of food safety, an accurate measurement is necessary. Test cubes of meat on the end and at the center to confirm that the entire kebab is properly cooked.

Of course, not all cuts of meat are going to simply lend themselves to be cut into perfect little 1-inch (2.5 cm) cubes. Chicken breasts in particular never cut right. No matter how careful items like this are cut, there are going to be thin, uneven, and just plain awkward pieces. However, the same rules apply: Uniformity and consistency of size are key to even cooking and a proper kebab. When it gets to these strangely shaped pieces, there are a few strategies. Rolling flaps of meat to create a useable shape is the easiest fix. Ultimately, proper carving for kebabs means cutting down to the size that you can get and not always the size the recipe calls for. Sometimes, you will need to adjust for the cut you have.

STRIPS: For tougher cuts of meat, strips are the better choice. Traditionally, dishes like Yakitori and satay are made from thin strips of meat threaded onto skewers. The best size for a strip of meat for this style of kebabs is approximately 1- to 1½-inches (2.5 to 4 cm) wide and no more than ¼-inch (6 mm) thick. Cut these strips to a length that accommodates the skewer being used. Generally, these strips should be about 4 to 6 inches (10 to 15 cm) in length. These kebabs cook very fast and should be cooked at the highest temperature possible. Turning the kebab over once is all that is necessary.

To thread a kebab of this type requires lacing the skewer through the meat a few times. Start with the strip of meat flat on a cutting board and push the skewer through the bottom of the strip about ½ inch (1.5 cm) from the bottom. To weave the meat onto the skewer properly, pass it back through the meat every 1 to 1½ inches (2.5 to 4 cm), repeating until you reach the top of the strip. Make sure that there is at least 1 inch (2.5 cm) of the skewer on either end of the strip of meat. A proper kebab of this type shouldn't flop around and should be stretched tightly on the skewer. Traditionally, bamboo skewers are used for this type of kebab because it grips the meat better. If using bamboo skewers, soak them in water for 30 minutes beforehand, keep them moist until they hit the grill, and use strips of aluminum foil laid flat on the grill to protect the ends from burning.

**MINCED OR GROUND MEATS:** Ground meat seems like a strange starting point for a kebab, but it has been used for centuries in dishes like koftas and seekh kebabs. The secret is to use a lean, good quality ground meat and to keep it dry, cold, and firm. For this style of kebabs, it is necessary to use broad, flat blade skewers or what are sometimes referred to as sword skewers. These should have a thin, flat blade that is at least ½-inch (1.5 cm) wide. The recipes of this style that we include in this book work from a mixture of meat, herbs, spices, and other ingredients. We have formulated these to produce a dry consistency in the meat, but a moist and tender product once grilled.

The minced meat used in these kebabs should be a fine grind, but avoid overworking the meat since it will tend to make it tough once cooked. The process for ground meat kebabs is to keep it cold right up to the moment it hits the grill. This means starting with the meat right out of the refrigerator, combining all the ingredients, and returning it to the refrigerator. Using clean and dry, flat blade skewers, form the meat into a sausage-like shape around the skewer. The kebab should be about 1 to 1¼ inches (2.5 to 3 cm) in diameter, about 6 to 8 inches (15 to 20 cm) in length, and consistent in thickness from end to end. Avoid tapering the meat towards the ends and make sure that the meat is tightly packed onto the skewer. Once formed, return to the refrigerator on a large platter or metal tray. It is vital that when cooking these kebabs that they sit flat on the cooking grates and that those grates be completely clean and well oiled.

**VEGETABLES:** When mixing meat and vegetables on a kebab (a perfectly good thing to do), it is important that the vegetables be cut to the size of the meat or slightly smaller. The whole point of grilling a kebab is to get a good charring on the surface. If the kebab is being held off the cooking grates by vegetables, then the meat will not get the flavor we are looking for, will take longer to cook, and will end up gray and flavorless. We cook the kebab to the doneness of the meat, not the doneness of the vegetables, so choose vegetables that are perfectly good undercooked and keep the pieces small.

Slices of onion and bell pepper should be threaded flat on the skewer. Frequently, these have a tendency to break when pushing the skewer through. To avoid this problem, lay the piece flat on a cutting board and press the skewer through the middle. If these are being used with cubes of beef, line them up to match the meat.

Vegetables like squash should be cut into rounds with the skins on. Once cooked, these can be too soft to stay on the skewer, so thread through the skin side, so that the cut side lies down on the grill. Vegetables like these will generally cook faster than meat, so cut them smaller than the meat cubes to lift them off the cooking surface and slow their cooking time.

# How to Grill a Kebab

Kebabs are easy. They are easy to prepare and easy to grill. For most people, the kebab is going to be cooked on a standard grill, whether gas or charcoal, and will sit directly on the cooking grates.

## OILING THE GRILL GRATES

To reduce the risk of the kebabs sticking, it is vital that the cooking grates be completely clean and well oiled. To oil a grill's cooking grate, preheat the grill to high. Grab hold of a wad of paper towels with a pair of long-handled tongs and dunk them in a small amount of cooking oil. Then swab the surface of the grill grates several times to create a nonstick surface. We recommend using a high smoke-point oil. Good oils to use include refined canola oil, avocado oil, and grapeseed oil. These oils can take the intense heat of the grill without breaking down and causing excessive smoke. As soon as the grates have been well oiled, the kebab should go on immediately.

## GRILLING TOOLS

The tool of choice for cooking kebabs is a good pair of long-handled metal-tipped tongs. This lets you get a grip on the food itself and control the skewers easily. A thin-blade spatula is also helpful. Some items may stick regardless of the precautions taken. A good spatula allows you to get under these pesky items and gently work them away from the cooking grates easily. We also recommend a good pair of heat-resistant gloves. Metal skewers can easily exceed 400 to 500°F (204 to 260°C) on the grill. Gloves, like the welding variety (which are better and cheaper than "grilling gloves"), allow for quick and easy handling of skewers. This is very helpful when doing a large number of kebabs.

## PATIENCE

Putting cold meat on a hot grill is like sticking your tongue on a frozen flagpole. It will stick. It will stick because the cold meat quickly cools the metal and that locks the two together. Once the food in contact with the metal cooks and begins to get a light charring, it will release. This is the exact moment to turn the kebabs. Fighting with stuck foods will tear apart the kebabs. Be patient and it will release.

When placing kebabs on the cooking grate, make sure that they are well supported. The best direction is diagonal to the cooking grates. This allows better access to the skewer, better support for the food, and an easy angle to work with. When turning kebabs, rotate them ninety degrees relative to the cooking grate to improve the evenness of the cooking. Cube kebabs can be turned on all four sides, strip kebabs should be flipped once, and minced kebabs can be gently rolled as they cook. With minced meat kebabs, it is important to take them slowly. This doesn't mean a low heat, but the meat needs to set up on the grill before it is turned. Moving too early can make them come apart on the grill. If this happens, don't panic. Using a pair of tongs, lay out the pieces to complete the grilling and remove as they finish cooking.

## CHARCOAL VERSUS GAS

It is the age-old question and to be honest, we do not care which one you use. A charcoal grill will give your kebabs a smokier, campfire flavor. Gas grills are, of course, easier to use and more convenient. Most people these days have gas grills. Both are perfect for grilling kebabs.

The only aspect of grilling that is different between grilling on charcoal versus gas has to do with the lid. For kebabs, it is perfectly fine to leave the lid up and not worry about this, but the general rule is that a charcoal grill is hotter with the lid off, while a gas grill is hotter with the lid down. Leave the lid up or off when grilling your kebabs, keep a close eye on them, and unless the recipe says otherwise, cook them hot and fast. This is the best method for kebabs.

## ELECTRIC AND INDOOR GRILLS

Electric grills, whether indoor or outdoor, as well as grill pans, work much more by contact cooking. This means that the food in contact with the surface will cook quickly, but the kebab as a whole will cook more slowly than on a gas or charcoal grill. As with other grills, a clean and oiled cooking surface is a must, but in general, these small grills work perfectly well for grilling kebabs.

# How to Serve a Kebab

Kebabs are a complete food item and can be served as is. It is important to note that if you intend to serve kebabs on the skewer, there needs to be enough room left on the end of the skewer for people to hold. Always leave a few inches (7.5 to 10 cm) of the skewer empty on the end so people can grab onto it. If using metal skewers, they can be very hot right off the grill. We are talking about a good 300°F (149°C) of heat, so to avoid burning people, either remove foods from the skewer before serving or allow the kebabs to cool for five to ten minutes before serving. Since it is best to serve most kebabs hot off the grill, it is important to remove the food from the skewer shortly after it's cooked through. This in no way detracts from the experience.

When handling hot kebabs, always use oven- or grill-safe gloves. Even bamboo can burn you if handled right off the grill. Use a fork to remove foods from a skewer.

Our favorite way to enjoy most of these kebab recipes in on flatbread or tortillas. Use the bread to grab a hold of the kebab. Carefully slide the contents off of skewer and *voila,* you have an instant sandwich, wrap, or taco.

# CHAPTER 1
# Beef Kebabs

- 20  Lebanese Beef Kofta
- 22  Balsamic-Brown Sugar Steak and Onion Kebabs
- 23  Meatball Kebab Subs
- 24  Peruvian Anticuchos
- 25  Carne Asada Kebabs
- 27  Steak and Potato Kebabs
- 28  Citrus-Horseradish Beef Kebabs
- 29  Steak and Mushroom Kebabs
- 30  Harissa Beef Kebabs
- 32  Beef Fajita Kebabs
- 33  West African Beef Kebabs (Suya Kebabs)
- 34  Beef Teriyaki Kebabs
- 36  Steakhouse Kebabs
- 37  Sesame Beef Kebabs
- 38  Beef Satay with Peanut Sauce
- 41  Chipotle-Adobo Beef Kebabs

Beef is a perfect meat for kebabs. It has the density to take the intense heat, sears well, and provides wide versatility. A great advantage of grilling beef on skewers is that generally, the best kebabs are not made from the most expensive cuts. Our favorite cuts of beef for kebabs are chuck roasts, boneless beef ribs, and tri-tip roasts. The quality to look for is a good ratio of fat to lean. It is the fat that keeps the meat moist. You do not want large chunks of fat, but plenty of small, marbled pieces of fat within the meat will add moistness and flavor. When working with large roasts, cut off and discard the gristle and the big hunks of fat. A large roast will provide the right size, shape, and quality of beef that best works in the recipes in this chapter. Avoid precut "stew meat" pieces found in supermarkets, since these are little more than discarded scraps of meat left over by the butcher.

While our recipes call for specific cuts of beef, feel free to substitute. It should be noted, however, that you will need to make some modifications. A beef cut that is well marbled may need nothing more than a good spice rub. A lean cut, like beef loin, tenderloin, or round and rump roasts, should spend some time in a marinade. The marinade not only tenderizes the meat but also to adds the necessary fat to make it flavorful. The volume needs to be enough to completely coat the meat. Place the marinade and the beef cubes or strips of beef in a resealable plastic bag with the marinade and refrigerate for two to four hours.

Overcooking beef will lead to a dry and tough kebab. There are certain precautions you can take to ensure a better kebab experience. First, make wise meat selections that work well with specific flavor profiles. Second, cutting the meat yourself, as opposed to letting the butcher cut it, allows you to get the proper meat-to-fat ratio. Third, take care to cook at the appropriate temperature: Some kebabs require a fast high-heat cook, while others benefit from a longer medium-heat cook.

Beef kebabs, with the exception of ground- or minced-meat kebabs, can be cooked to a level of doneness much like a steak. Ground meat must be cooked to 160°F (71°C) at all times. Cubes and strips of beef, like steaks, are perfectly safe at lower temperatures. We do not recommend a rare kebab, but medium rare is perfectly fine, and with some of these recipes, preferred.

# Lebanese Beef Kofta

MAKES 6 LARGE KEBABS

According to legend, the first hamburger was served at the St. Louis World's Fair in 1904. It was a ground beef patty, cooked on a flat griddle and put on a roll so it could be carried around while one enjoyed the exhibits. It's a great American story, but other cultures have also created portable ground beef dishes. Kofta originated in the East and predates written history, but it now is commonly found in Central Asia and across the Atlantic. While not shaped like a patty, there are some similarities. This skewered kebab is made from minced or ground meat, cooked over an open fire, and placed in a thick piece of flatbread like a pita for easy handling.

- 1½ pounds (680 g) ground chuck, preferably 85% lean
- 1 pound (455 g) ground beef sirloin, preferably 93% lean
- ½ cup (80 g) grated onion
- ¼ cup (15 g) finely chopped flat parsley
- 1¼ teaspoons salt
- 1 teaspoon ground cumin
- ½ teaspoon black pepper
- ½ teaspoon Aleppo pepper (substitute with red pepper flakes)
- ½ teaspoon ground coriander
- ¼ teaspoon sumac (substitute with citric acid)
- ¼ teaspoon cinnamon
- ¼ teaspoon allspice
- ¼ teaspoon ginger
- 6 large sword skewers
- Oil
- 1 lemon

**1.** Place the ground beef in a large bowl. Place the grated onion on a clean dish cloth, wring out the excess liquid, and add the onions to the bowl. Add the chopped parsley and all the spices to the beef and onion mixture.

**2.** Using your hands, gently combine all the ingredients, mixing but not overworking the meat. Cover the bowl with plastic wrap and place in the refrigerator for 30 minutes.

**3.** Form the beef into oblong koftas around each of the sword skewers. Each kofta kebab should be about 6 to 8 inches (15 to 20 cm) long. Make sure the meat is packed tightly around the skewer and that there is at least 1 inch (2.5 cm) of exposed metal on the end. Brush the surface with oil and return the uncooked koftas to the refrigerator, covered in plastic wrap, for 30 more minutes.

**4.** Preheat the grill for direct medium-high to high heat. When hot, oil the grill grates right before putting on the kebabs.

**5.** Place the koftas onto the grill. Leave the lid up and cook one side for 6 to 7 minutes, turn, and continue cooking until the internal temperature of the koftas reaches 160°F (71°C).

**6.** Remove the koftas from the grill and let them rest for 5 minutes. Gently slide them away from the skewers, place onto a clean platter, and squeeze lemon juice over top.

# Balsamic-Brown Sugar Steak and Onion Kebabs

MAKES 4 TO 6 KEBABS

The secret to these tender cubes of chuck roast is the glaze that caramelizes on the grill, thereby infusing a relatively cheap cut of beef with a deep rich flavor. This dish is perfect served over rice, quinoa, or pasta.

**KEBABS**
1 chuck roast (2 pounds, or 900 g)
1 medium sweet onion
4 to 6 skewers
2 tablespoons (28 ml) olive oil
1 teaspoon salt
½ teaspoon black pepper

**BASTE AND DIPPING SAUCE**
½ cup (120 ml) balsamic vinegar
3 tablespoons (45 ml) soy sauce
½ cup (115 g) dark brown sugar
¼ teaspoon mild or medium chili powder
⅛ teaspoon black pepper

**1.** In a medium saucepan, bring the balsamic vinegar and soy sauce to a boil. Add the brown sugar and stir. Reduce the burner to a low heat and simmer for 5 minutes. Watch that the sauce does not burn and stir occasionally. Add the chili powder and black pepper to the mixture. Simmer for an additional 2 to 3 minutes. The sauce should be able to coat the back of spoon. Remove the pan from the heat and let the mixture cool for 10 to 15 minutes before using. Once cooled, divide into two equal halves: use one half for a basting sauce and store the other half in a separate container in the refrigerator to be used as a dipping sauce when serving.

**2.** Cut away any excess fat from the chuck roast and cut into 1-inch (2.5 cm) cubes. Peel and cut the onion into 1-inch (2.5 cm) pieces.

**3.** Preheat the grill for high heat. When the grill is ready, oil the grill grates right before putting on the kebabs. Using long-handled tongs, dip some folded paper towels in a high smoke-point cooking oil and wipe down the grill grates, making at least three good passes to create a nonstick surface.

**4.** Thread the beef cubes and onion pieces onto the skewers, alternating between the two. Do not overcrowd the skewers. There should be between 5 to 8 pieces of meat per skewer, depending on its length. Brush both sides of the skewered meat and onions with olive oil and season well with the salt and black pepper.

**5.** Place the kebabs onto the grill. Cook for a total of 10 to 12 minutes, turning occasionally to expose each surface to the fire. After 5 minutes of cooking, begin basting the kebabs with the basting sauce.

**6.** Once the beef is cooked to the desired doneness, remove the kebabs from the grill and serve with the warmed reserved dipping sauce.

---

**NOTE:** For a vegetarian or vegan option, substitute firm tofu, plain seitan, or cremini or portabella mushrooms for the beef.

# Meatball Kebab Subs

MAKES 6 KEBABS

This is one of the easiest and most convenient ways to prepare a meatball sub sandwich. Think of it as the cookout, camping, or tailgater's version of a stovetop favorite. The meatball kebabs cook quickly and really benefit from that open flame flavor.

**KEBABS**
1 cup (50 g) cubed day old bread
¼ (60 ml) cup milk
2 pounds (900 g) ground beef (85% lean)
¼ cup (25 g) grated Parmesan cheese
1 egg, lightly beaten
3 cloves of garlic, minced
2 teaspoons dried basil
1 teaspoon dried oregano
1½ teaspoons salt
½ teaspoon black pepper
¼ teaspoon red pepper flakes
6 skewers

**FOR SERVING**
6 sub sandwich buns (6 inches, or 15 cm each)
3 cups (750 g) prepared marinara sauce
6 or 12 slices of provolone cheese

**1.** Soak the bread cubes in milk for 15 minutes. Squeeze out the excess milk and set the soaked bread aside. Discard the milk.

**2.** Combine the ground beef with the soaked bread, Parmesan cheese, egg, garlic, basil, oregano, salt, black pepper, and red pepper flakes. Form the mixture into 1½-inch (4 cm) meatballs. Thread 3 to 4 meatballs onto each skewer. Do not overcrowd. Make sure that the meatballs are compact enough to stay on the skewer.

**3.** Preheat the grill for medium-high heat. When the grill is ready, oil the grill grates right before putting on the kebabs. Using long-handled tongs, dip some folded paper towels in a high smoke-point cooking oil and wipe down the grill grates, making at least three good passes to create a nonstick surface.

**4.** Place the kebabs onto the grill. Cook for 3 minutes. Gently turn and cook for another 2 to 3 minutes. Repeat the process until all surfaces are well browned and the internal temperature of meatballs reaches 160°F (71°C).

**5.** Remove the kebabs from the grill and slide into warmed sandwich buns. Remove the skewers from the meatballs. Top each sandwich with hot marinara sauce and sliced provolone cheese.

# Peruvian Anticuchos

MAKES 6 KEBABS

This recipe is traditionally made with beef heart, but for the purposes of this cookbook we will use a more familiar meat instead. If you have access to beef heart and want to try it, by all means do. The main flavor component is a smoky chile pepper paste often used in Peruvian cooking called Aji Panca. It can be a little hard to find in a regular grocery store, but is readily available online and in South American specialty food stores. If you don't have time to track it down, then see the instructions for a suitable replacement.

**KEBABS**

1½ pounds (680 g) chuck roast or boneless short ribs
6 skewers

**MARINADE**

⅓ cup (27 g) Aji Panca paste
¼ cup (60 ml) white wine vinegar
4 to 6 cloves of garlic
1 tablespoon (7 g) ground cumin
1¼ teaspoons salt
1 teaspoon dried oregano
½ teaspoon black pepper

**1.** Place the ingredients for the marinade in food processor. Pulse 7 to 8 times. If you do not have access to Aji Panca, simply soak 4 dried pasilla peppers in warm water for 30 minutes and then drain the peppers, cut off the stems, and remove the seeds. Roughly chop the peppers and add to the food processor with the remaining ingredients plus 1 to 2 tablespoons (15 to 28 ml) water for a thinner consistency.

**2.** Remove any excess fat from the beef and cut into 1¼-inch (3 cm) cubes.

**3.** Place the beef cubes into a resealable plastic bag. Pour the marinade over the beef and toss gently to coat. Remove any excess air from the bag, seal, and place into the refrigerator for 12 to 24 hours.

**4.** Preheat the grill for medium-high heat. When the grill is ready, oil the grill grates right before putting on the kebabs. Using long-handled tongs, dip some folded paper towels in a high smoke-point cooking oil and wipe down the grill grates, making at least three good passes to create a nonstick surface.

**5.** Thread the marinated beef cubes onto the skewers. Discard any marinade remaining in the bag.

**6.** Place the kebabs onto the grill. Cook for 10 to 12 minutes, turning two to three times during cooking process.

**7.** Remove the kebabs from the grill and serve.

NOTE: For a vegetarian or vegan option, use plain cubed seitan instead of beef.

# Carne Asada Kebabs

MAKES 15 TO 20 KEBABS

The secret to making these kebabs is to cut the meat into very thin strips. We choose tri-tip for this one because it has a perfect balance of lean to fat so that the beef is flavorful and tender, provided it is cooked quickly. This kebab is perfect for tacos and can be removed quickly form the skewer and go straight to a warmed tortilla in no time.

**KEBABS**
1 tri-tip roast (3 pounds, or 1.3 kg)
15 to 20 skewers (presoak if using bamboo skewers)

**MARINADE**
Juice of 3 limes
⅓ cup (80 ml) tequila
¼ cup (60 ml) vegetable oil
2 cloves of garlic, minced
2 teaspoons onion powder
2 teaspoons salt
1 teaspoon ground cumin
1 teaspoon black pepper

1. Combine all the ingredients for the marinade in a small bowl.

2. Slice the tri-tip roast into 4 x 1 to 1½-inch (10 x 2.5 to 4 cm) strips.

3. Place the beef strips into a resealable plastic bag. Pour the marinade over the beef and toss gently to coat. Release any air from the bag, seal, and place into the refrigerator for 4 to 6 hours.

4. Preheat the grill for high heat. When the grill is ready, oil the grill grates right before putting on the kebabs. Using long-handled tongs, dip some folded paper towels in a high smoke-point cooking oil and wipe down the grill grates, making at least three good passes to create a nonstick surface.

5. Thread the marinated meat onto the skewers by weaving the skewer through the strip of meat. The beef strip should by laid out thin along the length of the skewer. Discard any marinade remaining in the bag.

6. Place the kebabs onto the grill. Cook for 3 minutes per side.

7. Once the beef is cooked to the desired doneness, remove the kebabs from the grill. Remove the meat from the skewers and serve immediately in warmed tortillas.

> NOTE: For a vegetarian or vegan option, use tempeh, large pieces of firm tofu, or portabella mushroom strips instead of beef.

# Steak and Potato Kebabs

MAKES 6 TO 8 KEBABS

Who doesn't love steak and potatoes? It is a very popular food combination eaten in the West. This is the kebab version of that dish. It is best to parboil the potatoes before placing them on the skewer. That way, the steak and potatoes cook evenly and at the same rate. Look for very tiny potatoes. If you cannot find them, try using smaller fingerling potatoes.

**2 pounds (900 g) sirloin or tri-tip steaks**
**20 to 22 tiny potatoes, 1 to 1½ inches (2.5 to 4 cm) around**
**6 to 8 skewers**
**Olive oil**
**1 teaspoon black pepper**
**2½ teaspoons (45 g) salt**
**½ teaspoon dried marjoram**

**1.** Parboil the potatoes for 6 to 8 minutes, depending on their size. The potatoes should be tender, but not mushy. They will finish cooking on the grill. When the potatoes have reached the desired doneness, remove them from the pot and place into an ice bath (a bowl filled with cold water and ice) for 5 minutes to stop the cooking process. Remove the potatoes from the ice bath and pat dry. Set aside.

**2.** Cut the steaks into 1¼-inch (3 cm) cubes.

**3.** Preheat the grill for medium-high heat. When the grill is ready, oil the grill grates right before putting on the kebabs. Using long-handled tongs, dip some folded paper towels in a high smoke-point cooking oil and wipe down the grill grates, making at least three good passes to create a nonstick surface.

**4.** Thread the beef cubes onto the skewers, alternating with the parboiled potatoes. Brush the kebabs with olive oil and mix together the black pepper, salt, and dried marjoram. Season the kebabs well with the mixture.

**5.** Place the kebabs onto the grill. Cook for 4 minutes, gently turn, and cook for a remaining 5 minutes or until meat has reached desired doneness and the potatoes have cooked all the way through.

**6.** Remove the kebabs from the grill and serve.

> **NOTE:** For a vegetarian or vegan option, use mushrooms or seitan instead of the beef. Reduce the cooking time by half.

# Citrus-Horseradish Beef Kebabs

MAKES 6 TO 8 KEBABS

Citrus and horseradish work really well together, and this combination is brilliant on a large beef roast. Here, we have adapted this flavor combination into a smaller package. These kebabs are tender, sweet, savory, and of course, peppery.

**KEBABS**
1½ to 2 pounds (680 to 900 g) beef sirloin
6 to 8 skewers
1½ teaspoons salt
1 teaspoon black pepper

**MARINADE AND BASTE**
1 teaspoon oil
3 cloves of garlic, minced
1 cup (250 g) prepared barbecue sauce
½ cup (160 g) orange marmalade
2½ tablespoons (38 g) prepared horseradish
Juice of 1 lime
¼ teaspoon cayenne pepper

**1.** Heat the oil in a medium saucepan and sauté the garlic for 30 seconds until fragrant. Add the remaining marinade and baste ingredients. Simmer on medium-low for 5 minutes. Remove from the heat and let cool for 15 minutes. Divide the sauce in half, using one half as a marinade and reserving the other half in a separate container in the refrigerator to use as a basting sauce. Rewarm the basting sauce in the microwave for 30 to 60 seconds before using.

**2.** Cut the beef sirloin into 1¼-inch (3 cm) cubes.

**3.** Place the beef cubes into a resealable plastic bag. Pour the marinade over the beef and toss gently to coat. Release any excess air from the bag, seal, and place into the refrigerator for 4 to 12 hours.

**4.** Preheat the grill for medium-high heat. When the grill is ready, oil the grill grates. Using long-handled tongs, dip some folded paper towels in a high smoke-point cooking oil and wipe down the grill grates, making at least three good passes to create a nonstick surface.

**5.** Thread the marinated beef cubes onto the skewers. Season with salt and pepper on both sides.

**6.** Place the kebabs on grill. Cook for a total of 10 to 12 minutes. Baste with the warmed reserved basting sauce after the first 5 minutes of cooking. Baste, turn, and then baste again. Repeat this process 2 to 3 times until well coated. Watch for burning; move the kebabs to a cooler part of the grill or reduce the heat if necessary.

**7.** Once the beef is cooked to the desired doneness, remove the kebabs from the grill and place onto a clean platter. Lightly cover with aluminum foil and let the meat rest for at least 5 minutes before serving.

> **NOTE:** For a vegetarian or vegan option, use portabella mushrooms, eggplant, or firm tofu instead of the beef.

# Steak and Mushroom Kebabs

MAKES 6 TO 8 KEBABS

Consider this the quick and easy way to put a classic steakhouse meal on a skewer. In addition to the benefit of being on a skewer, this dish also has a deep richness from the boneless sort rib that results in a hearty finished product you'd expect from any restaurant steak. What's the added bonus? It's a much less expensive alternative and equally as delicious.

**KEBABS**

1½ pounds (680 g) boneless beef short ribs
12 ounces (340 g) white mushrooms
6 to 8 skewers
¼ cup (60 ml) vegetable oil

**SPICE RUB**

2 teaspoons salt
1 teaspoon onion powder
½ teaspoon black pepper
¼ teaspoon sweet paprika
¼ cup (50 g) white sugar

**1.** Clean the mushrooms with a damp cloth or several dampened paper towels. If using bamboo skewers, make sure to soak them in tepid water for 15 minutes.

**2.** Cut the beef short ribs into 1- to 1¼-inch (2.5 to 3 cm) cubes.

**3.** Preheat the grill for high heat. When the grill is ready, oil the grill grates right before putting on the kebabs. Using long-handled tongs, dip some folded paper towels in a high smoke-point cooking oil and wipe down the grill grates, making at least three good passes to create a nonstick surface.

**4.** Combine all the ingredients for the spice rub.

**5.** Thread the beef cubes and mushrooms onto the skewers, alternating between the two, starting and finishing with beef. Leave at least ½ to ¾ inch (1.5 to 2 cm) of exposed skewer in the front. Do not overcrowd. Brush the kebabs on both sides with vegetable oil. Sprinkle evenly with the spice rub.

**6.** Place the kebabs onto the grill. Cook for a total of 12 minutes, turning a few times during the cooking process.

**7.** Once the beef is cooked to the desired doneness and the mushrooms take on a deep color, remove the kebabs from the grill.

NOTE: For a vegetarian or vegan option, use plain seitan or all mushrooms.

# Harissa Beef Kebabs

MAKES 8 KEBABS

These flavorful Moroccan-style kebabs have a mild smokiness attributed to its North African flavor profile. Serve with warmed flatbread, yogurt sauce, and rice pilaf.

**KEBABS**

2 pounds (900 g) sirloin steak
2 red bell peppers
8 skewers

**MARINADE**

1 tablespoon (6 g) cumin seeds
2 teaspoons caraway seeds
1½ teaspoons black peppercorns
¼ cup (60 ml) olive oil
1 small shallot, minced
2 to 3 cloves of garlic, minced
1 tablespoon (15 ml) white vinegar
1½ teaspoons salt
1 teaspoon smoked paprika
¼ teaspoon cayenne pepper

**1.** Toast the cumin seeds, caraway seeds, and peppercorns in a small skillet until they become fragrant, about 1 to 2 minutes. Make sure to move them around the pan so they don't burn. Remove from the heat and place into a spice (or coffee) grinder and pulverize. Place into a bowl. Add the remaining ingredients for the marinade and mix well. Set aside while you prepare the meat.

**2.** Cut the sirloin into 1¼-inch (3 cm) cubes.

**3.** Place the beef cubes into a resealable plastic bag. Pour the marinade over the beef and toss gently to coat. Remove any excess air from the bag, seal, and place into the refrigerator for 6 to 8 hours.

**4.** Preheat the grill for medium-high heat. When the grill is ready, oil the grill grates right before putting on the kebabs. Using long-handled tongs, dip some folded paper towels in a high smoke-point cooking oil and wipe down the grill grates, making at least three good passes to create a nonstick surface.

**5.** Core and cut the bell peppers into 1¼-inch (3 cm) pieces.

**6.** Thread the marinated beef cubes and bell pepper pieces onto the skewers, alternating between the two. Discard any marinade remaining in the bowl. Place the kebabs on the grill. Cook for 11 to 13 minutes, turning a ¼ turn every 2 to 3 minutes.

**7.** Once the beef is cooked to the desired doneness, remove the kebabs from the grill and serve.

> **NOTE:** For a vegetarian or vegan option, use seitan, firm tofu, or vegetables such as mushrooms, additional bell peppers, and onions.

# Beef Fajita Kebabs

MAKES 6 TO 8 KEBABS

Beef fajitas are an old favorite. These kebabs are great for large gatherings but easy enough for a small family dinner. Simply serve in warmed tortillas with sour cream and a fresh batch of homemade guacamole. All you need to do it grab the kebab with the tortilla and pull the beef, bell peppers, and onions right off.

**KEBABS**

1 chuck roast (2½ pounds, or 1 kg)
2 green bell peppers
1 red onion
6 to 8 skewers

**MARINADE**

1 cup (235 ml) flat beer (ale is preferred)
⅓ cup (80 ml) lime juice
¼ cup (60 ml) vegetable oil
3 cloves of garlic, minced
2½ teaspoons (6 g) ground cumin
2 teaspoons salt
1½ teaspoons mild chili powder
½ teaspoon black pepper

**FOR SERVING**

8 to 12 warmed tortillas
1 cup (225 g) guacamole
¾ cup (180 g) sour cream

1. Combine all the ingredients for the marinade.

2. Cut off any excess pieces of fat from the chuck roast and cut into 1¼-inch (3 cm) cubes.

3. Place the beef cubes into a plastic bowl or resealable plastic bag. Pour the marinade over the beef and toss gently to coat. Cover the bowl or seal the bag and place into the refrigerator for 6 to 12 hours.

4. Preheat the grill for medium-high heat. When the grill is ready, oil the grill grates right before putting on the kebabs. Using long-handled tongs, dip some folded paper towels in a high smoke-point cooking oil and wipe down the grill grates, making at least three good passes to create a nonstick surface.

5. Core and cut the bell pepper into 1¼-inch (3 cm) pieces. Peel and cut up the onions into 1¼-inch (3 cm) pieces.

6. Thread the marinated beef cubes, bell peppers, and onions onto the skewers in the following order: beef, bell pepper, onion, beef, bell pepper, onion, and so on. Discard any marinade remaining in the bowl.

7. Place the kebabs onto the grill. Cook for 12 minutes or so. Meanwhile, wrap some tortillas in aluminum foil. Place onto the cool side of the grill. Turn a few times during the cooking process.

8. Once the beef is cooked to the desired doneness, remove the kebabs and the packet of tortillas from the grill. Place the kebabs on a platter. Using kitchen gloves, carefully open the aluminum packet and transfer the tortillas to a tortilla warmer or cover with a clean kitchen towel. Serve with sour cream and guacamole.

# West African Beef Kebabs (Suya Kebabs)

MAKES 15 TO 20 KEBABS

These kebabs are similar in presentation to satay sticks, but are spicier and call for ground peanuts or almonds in the spice rub. Serve these kebabs as an appetizer or at a cocktail party. These spicy bite-sized morsels go down well with a glass of wine or an ice cold beer.

**KEBABS**

1½ pounds (680 g) flat iron steak
15 to 20 skewers
⅓ to ½ cup (80 to 120 ml) oil

**SPICE RUB**

⅓ cup (48 g) roasted peanuts
2½ teaspoons (5 g) cayenne pepper
1½ teaspoons salt
1 teaspoon garlic powder
1 teaspoon onion powder
½ teaspoon black pepper
¼ teaspoon cinnamon

**1.** Place the peanuts into a food processor and pulse until you achieve a meal-like consistency. Place into a bowl with the remaining ingredients for the spice rub. Transfer to a large tray and spread the mixture out evenly.

**2.** Cut the flat iron steak into 3½- to 4-inch (9 to 10 cm) long strips that are 1¼-inch (3 cm) wide and ¾-inch (2 cm) thick.

**3.** Thread one piece of beef onto each skewer in a weaving pattern.

**4.** Preheat the grill for medium-high heat. When the grill is ready, oil the grill grates right before putting on the kebabs. Using long-handled tongs, dip some folded paper towels in a high smoke-point cooking oil and wipe down the grill grates, making at least three good passes to create a nonstick surface.

**5.** Brush both sides of the kebabs with oil. This will help the seasonings to adhere. Immediately dip both sides of the kebabs into the tray containing the spice rub. Set onto a clean plate. Repeat the process until all the kebabs are coated with the spice rub.

**6.** Place the kebabs onto the grill. You might have to do this in batches. Cook for about 2 to 3 minutes per side.

**7.** Once the beef is cooked to the desired doneness, remove the kebabs from the heat immediately and serve.

> **NOTE:** For a vegetarian or vegan option, use long strips of firm tofu or zucchini instead of the beef.

# Beef Teriyaki Kebabs

MAKES 6 TO 8 KEBABS

The secret to a great beef teriyaki isn't in the sauce, though that is also important. It is in the cut of beef. Boneless beef ribs provide the perfect lean-to-fat ratio resulting in a tender and flavorful kebab. The added bonus is that beef short ribs come in easy-to-handle strips that make preparing these kebabs quick and easy.

**KEBABS**

1 pound (455 g) boneless beef short ribs
1 large bell pepper
1 small red onion
10 to 12 small white mushrooms, cleaned
6 to 8 skewers
½ teaspoon salt
½ teaspoon white pepper
2 medium green onions, green portion only, finely chopped (for garnish)

**TERIYAKI SAUCE**

½ cup (120 ml) soy sauce
¼ cup (85 g) honey
¼ cup (60 g) dark brown sugar
1 tablespoon (15 g) oyster sauce
1 tablespoon (15 ml) mirin (substitute with sherry)
1 teaspoon red wine vinegar
1 teaspoon grated ginger
⅛ teaspoon salt
2 tablespoons (28 ml) water
1 teaspoon cornstarch

**1.** Combine all the ingredients for the Teriyaki Sauce, except for the water and cornstarch, in a saucepan over medium heat. Simmer for 5 to 6 minutes until the sugar and honey are completely dissolved. Stir occasionally and watch that the Teriyaki Sauce does not burn. Reduce the heat if necessary. Dissolve the cornstarch completely in the water and add to the saucepan. Stir to incorporate. Cook for 1 to 2 minutes more until the sauce has thickened enough to coat the back of a spoon. Remove from the heat. If serving the kebabs as part of a teriyaki bowl, double the Teriyaki Sauce recipe, divide the finished sauce in half, and reserve one half in a separate container in the refrigerator to be used when serving.

**2.** Cut the boneless beef short ribs into 1-inch (2.5 cm) cubes. Core and cut the bell pepper into 1-inch (2.5 cm) pieces. Peel and cut the onion into 1-inch (2.5 cm) pieces.

**3.** Preheat the grill for medium-high direct heat. When the grill is ready, oil the grill grates right before putting on the kebabs. Using long-handled tongs, dip some folded paper towels in a high smoke-point cooking oil and wipe down the grill grates, making at least three good passes to create a nonstick surface.

**4.** Thread the beef cubes, mushrooms, onion, and bell pepper onto the skewers in the following order: begin with bell pepper, then meat, mushrooms, meat, onion, meat, and end with bell pepper. Season the kebabs with salt and white pepper.

**5.** Place the kebabs onto the grill. Cook for total of 10 minutes. Brush with the Teriyaki Sauce continuously throughout the cooking process.

**6.** Once the beef is cooked to the desired doneness, remove the kebabs from the grill and serve with chopped green onion.

NOTE: For a vegetarian or vegan option, simply omit the beef and double up on the vegetables.

# Steakhouse Kebabs

MAKES 6 TO 8 KEBABS

These sirloin steak kebabs are served with a flavorful steak sauce. It's reminiscent of kebabs served in steakhouses all over the United States.

### KEBABS
2 pounds (900 g) sirloin steaks
6 to 8 skewers

### SPICE RUB
1½ teaspoons salt
1½ teaspoons black pepper
½ teaspoon Hungarian paprika (or sweet paprika)
½ teaspoon onion powder

### STEAK SAUCE
¼ cup (40 g) grated onion
2 teaspoons olive oil
1 clove of garlic, minced
¾ cup (180 g) ketchup
2 tablespoons (28 ml) water
2 tablespoons (28 ml) Worcestershire sauce
2 tablespoons (28 ml) white vinegar
1½ tablespoons (25 ml) soy sauce
2 tablespoons (30 g) brown sugar
1 tablespoon (11 g) yellow mustard
⅛ teaspoon salt
⅛ teaspoon black pepper

**1.** Grate the onion and place into a clean dish towel. Wring out any excess liquid and set aside.

**2.** Heat 2 teaspoons of olive oil in a medium saucepan. Add the grated onion and cook over medium heat for 2 minutes until translucent. Add the garlic and cook for 15 to 30 seconds. Add the remaining ingredients, stir, and bring to a medium simmer for 2 to 3 minutes. Stir often. Remove from the heat and set aside.

**3.** Cut the sirloin steaks into 1¼-inch (3 cm) cubes.

**4.** Thread the steak cubes onto the skewers. Brush both sides of the kebabs with olive oil.

**5.** Combine all the ingredients for the spice rub and season the kebabs well.

**6.** Preheat the grill for medium-high heat. When the grill is ready, oil the grill grates right before putting on the kebabs. Using long-handled tongs, dip some folded paper towels in a high smoke-point cooking oil and wipe down the grill grates, making at least three good passes to create a nonstick surface.

**7.** Place the kebabs onto the grill. Cook for 5 to 6 minutes per side or until they reach desired doneness. Some will cook faster than others. Simply move to a cooler part of grill or take off and set onto a clean platter until the remaining kebabs have cooked through.

**8.** Once the beef is cooked to the desired doneness, remove the kebabs from the grill. Serve the kebabs with warmed Steak Sauce on the side.

> **NOTE:** For a vegetarian or vegan option, substitute seitan, firm tofu, or mushrooms for the steak. Reduce the cooking time to 2 to 3 minutes per side.

# Sesame Beef Kebabs

MAKES 6 TO 8 KEBABS

Korean sesame beef is traditionally made with butterflied short ribs and served in lettuce with condiments. This is the kebab version of that dish. All you need are whole lettuce leaves, diced chilies, and a good appetite.

**KEBABS**
2 pounds (900 g) boneless short ribs
1 sweet onion
6 to 8 skewers
2 tablespoons (16 g) toasted sesame seeds (for garnish)

**MARINADE**
½ cup (120 ml) soy sauce
¼ cup (85 g) honey
1½ tablespoons (25 ml) sesame oil
1 tablespoon (15 ml) dry sherry
2 to 3 cloves of garlic
1 teaspoon grated ginger
1 teaspoon white pepper
½ teaspoon onion powder
¼ teaspoon red pepper flakes

1. Combine all the ingredients for the marinade.

2. Cut the short ribs into 1-inch (2.5 cm) cubes.

3. Place the beef cubes into a resealable plastic bag. Pour the marinade over the beef and toss gently to coat. Remove any excess air from the bag, seal, and place into the refrigerator for 4 to 6 hours.

4. Peel and cut the sweet onion into 1-inch (2.5 cm) pieces.

5. Thread the marinated beef cubes and onion pieces onto the skewers, alternating between the two. Place the kebabs onto a large cookie sheet. Discard any marinade remaining in the bag.

6. Preheat the grill for medium-high heat. When the grill is ready, oil the grill grates right before putting on the kebabs. Using long-handled tongs, dip some folded paper towels in a high smoke-point cooking oil and wipe down the grill grates, making at least three good passes to create a nonstick surface.

7. Place the kebabs onto the grill. Cook for 10 to 12 minutes. Do not turn the kebabs too soon once they hit the grill. Let them cook for at least 3 minutes before attempting to turn.

8. Once the beef is cooked to the desired doneness, remove the kebabs from the grill. Place onto a clean platter and top with toasted sesame seeds. You may also remove them from the skewers before garnishing. Serve over rice or as part of a lettuce wrap.

**NOTE:** For a vegetarian or vegan option, use portabella mushroom pieces instead of the meat and marinate for 1 hour.

# Beef Satay with Peanut Sauce

MAKES 15 TO 20 KEBABS

Satay is the kebab of choice of Indonesia. This popular dish has spread throughout the world and can be made using any meat, so feel free to try this recipe with chicken, pork, turkey, or anything else you can find. What makes this a particular favorite is the Peanut Sauce used for dipping. It has sweet, heat, salt, and savory all bundled up in one.

**KEBABS**

2 pounds (900 g) flat iron or flank steak
15 to 20 skewers

**MARINADE**

⅓ cup (80 ml) soy sauce
3 tablespoons (3 g) chopped cilantro (coriander leaves)
1 tablespoon (15 ml) white wine vinegar
1 tablespoon (5 g) minced lemongrass
1 tablespoon (15 g) brown sugar
2 teaspoons fish sauce
3 cloves of garlic
1 teaspoon ground turmeric
1 teaspoon grated ginger
½ teaspoon black pepper
⅛ teaspoon salt

**PEANUT SAUCE**

½ cup (130 g) smooth peanut butter
¼ cup (60 ml) soy sauce
2 tablespoons (28 ml) tepid water
1 tablespoon (15 g) brown sugar
1 teaspoon Asian chili paste
1 clove of garlic, minced

**1.** Combine all the ingredients for the marinade.

**2.** Cut the beef into 3- to 4-inch (7.5 to 10 cm) long strips that are 1-inch (2.5 cm) wide and ¾-inch (2 cm) thick.

**3.** Place the beef strips into a resealable bag or shallow dish. Pour the marinade over the beef and toss gently to coat. Remove any excess air from the bag, seal, and place into the refrigerator for 4 hours.

**4.** Combine all the ingredients for the Peanut Sauce in a medium bowl. Check for consistency. Add more water if the mixture is too thick. Also, you can add more chili paste if desired. Cover with plastic and place into refrigerator. Remove and let stand at room temperature at least 1 hour before serving.

**5.** Preheat the grill for high heat. When the grill is ready, oil the grill grates right before putting on the kebabs. Using long-handled tongs, dip some folded paper towels in a high smoke-point cooking oil and wipe down the grill grates, making at least three good passes to create a nonstick surface.

**6.** Thread one piece of marinated beef onto each skewer in a weaving pattern. Discard any marinade remaining in the bag.

**7.** Place the kebabs onto the grill. Cook for a total of 5 to 6 minutes, 3 minutes per side.

**8.** Once cooked, remove the kebabs from the grill and serve with the Peanut Sauce.

> **NOTE:** For a vegetarian or vegan option, use plain cubed seitan or tofu instead of the beef.

# Chipotle-Adobo Beef Kebabs

MAKES 6 TO 8 KEBABS

Spicy, delicious and versatile, these kebabs are reminiscent of some Mexican fast casual dining offerings. Serve these flavorful kebabs as appetizers, over rice, on simply slide into warmed tortillas. Use boneless beef short ribs for this recipe. Ask your local butcher for help locating the right cut. It will be well worth the effort.

**KEBABS**
Boneless beef short ribs (2 to 2½ pounds, or 900 g to 1 kg)
6 to 8 skewers

**MARINADE**
1 can (7 ounces, or 200 g) of chipotle in adobo
½ onion, roughly chopped
2 to 3 cloves garlic
½ cup (120 ml) beef broth
1 tablespoon (15 ml) white vinegar
1½ teaspoon salt
1 teaspoon ground cumin
½ teaspoon dried oregano
½ teaspoon black pepper

**1.** Place all the ingredients for the marinade into a food processor and pulse 10 or so times.

**2.** Cut the short ribs into 1¼-inch (3 cm) cubes.

**3.** Place the cubed short ribs into a resealable plastic bag. Pour the marinade over the beef and toss gently to coat. Remove any excess air from the bag, seal, and place into the refrigerator for 4 to 6 hours. The longer it marinates, the better it will be, but for no longer than 8 hours.

**4.** Preheat the grill for medium-high heat. When the grill is ready, oil the grill grates right before putting on the kebabs. Using long-handled tongs, dip some folded paper towels in a high smoke-point cooking oil and wipe down the grill grates, making at least three good passes to create a nonstick surface.

**5.** Thread the marinated beef cubes onto the skewers, place onto a large baking sheet, and brush with some of the marinade from the bag. Discard any remaining marinade.

**6.** Place the kebabs onto the grill. Cook for 10 to 12 minutes, turning 3 to 4 times during the cooking process.

**7.** Once the beef is cooked to the desired doneness (we recommend 145°F [63°C] and above), remove the kebabs from the grill and serve.

> **NOTE:** For a vegetarian or vegan option, use firm tofu, plain seitan, or tempeh instead of the beef.

# CHAPTER 2
# Pork and Lamb Kebabs

- 44 Pork Souvlaki
- 45 Kansas City Pork Kebabs
- 46 Vietnamese Pork Meatballs (Nem Nuang)
- 49 Fig and Pork Tenderloin Kebabs
- 50 Filipino Pork Kebabs
- 51 Pork Pinchos (Spanish Pork Kebabs)
- 52 Pork Belly Kebabs with Plum Glaze
- 54 Cumin-Blood Orange Pork Kebabs
- 55 Sweet and Sour Pork Kebabs
- 56 Pork Kebabs with Mustard BBQ Sauce
- 58 Hawaiian SPAM and Pineapple Kebabs
- 59 Maple-Sage Pork Kebabs
- 61 Bratwurst, Onion, and Bell Pepper Kebabs
- 62 Greek Lamb Kebabs
- 63 Lamb Shish Kebabs
- 64 Spicy Lamb Skewers (Yang Rou Chuan)
- 66 Pomegranate-Mint Lamb Kebabs
- 67 Seekh Kebabs
- 69 Sosaties (Lamb and Apricot Kebabs)
- 70 Jalapeño, Mint, and Red Onion Lamb Kebabs
- 71 Gyro Meatballs with Feta Tzatziki Sauce

Pork tenderloin is a great cut for kebabs. It is, however, not the optimal cut. The secret to making superior kebabs is the right combination of fat to lean, and the pork butt has a better quantity of fat. Also, it comes in a medium to large rectangular block, and despite the large bone that runs through the middle, it is easy to cut into cubes. We recommend getting a 3-pound (1.5 kg) pork butt. Once the fat is trimmed, there will be 2 to 2½ pounds (900 g to 1 kg) of meat left.

Pork tenderloin is our second choice. It is lean, very tender, and full of flavor. The secret is to grill hot and fast and not to overcook it. Pork is done and safe to consume at 145°F (63°C). This is always the target temperature for pork kebabs, unless they call for ground pork, then, as with all ground meat, the finished cooking temperature must be above 160°F (71°C). The best solution to prevent leaner cuts from drying out is to use a brine. Use the recipe found on page 12. Avoid substituting tenderloin with the less expensive pork loin. Pork loin lacks tenderness, internal fat, and the flavor necessary to make the most of our kebabs. Also, avoid purchasing chops, which are more expensive because the butcher had to cut them, and precut pork, which contains leftover scraps.

Lamb, one of our favorite meats, has the flavor that stands out to make it one of the best meats to hit the grill, regardless of preparation. Lamb has become very expensive, however, and availability can be sparse. Turning lamb into kebabs is a way to stretch the investment by making more meal with less meat. Although lamb shoulder is one of the best cuts for kebabs, it tends to get trimmed down into shoulder chops, which, if they are thick enough, is a good option. Unfortunately, finding them cut an inch (2.5 cm) in thickness can be hit or miss. So as we always say, talk to your butcher. When we can't find good lamb shoulder, we generally choose leg of lamb for making kebabs. Buying it whole, either bone in or boneless, means doing some trimming, but with practice it can be done quickly. The ratio of fat to meat in both leg of lamb and lamb shoulder is excellent and the flavor superior.

Lamb is done and safe to consume at 145°F (63°C), which is medium rare. For ground lamb, the internal safe temperature is 160°F (71°C). In most cases for lamb cubes, it is perfectly fine to cook to higher temperatures, up to 165°F (74°C) for well done, without it becoming too tough and dry. However, we recommend the lower temperature to maximize flavor and tenderness.

# Pork Souvlaki

MAKES 4 TO 6 KEBABS

The classic souvlaki sticks available at fast food joints and street carts are often tough and dry, which is a real shame. The problem is lean pork. Opt instead for pork butt, or as it is sometimes called, Boston roast; this cut has a little more fat and a lot more flavor. These kebabs won't be greasy, but they will be tender and delicious.

**KEBABS**
1 pork butt (2 pounds, or 900 g)
4 to 6 skewers

**MARINADE**
Juice of 2 large lemons
¼ cup (60 ml) olive oil
¼ cup (16 g) loosely packed fresh oregano leaves, finely chopped
3 cloves of garlic, minced
1 tablespoon (15 ml) red wine vinegar
1¼ teaspoons salt
½ teaspoon black pepper

**FOR SERVING**
Pita bread
Tzatziki sauce
Chopped onions
Sliced tomatoes

**1.** Combine all the ingredients for the marinade.

**2.** Remove any excess fat from the pork roast and cut into 1- to 1¼- inch (2.5 to 3 cm) cubes.

**3.** Place the pork cubes into a resealable plastic bag or a large bowl. Pour the marinade over the pork and toss gently to coat. Seal the bag or cover the bowl and place into the refrigerator for 4 hours.

**4.** Preheat the grill for medium-high heat. When the grill is ready, oil the grill grates right before putting on the kebabs. Using long-handled tongs, dip some folded paper towels in a high smoke point cooking oil and wipe down the grill grates, making at least three good passes to create a nonstick surface.

**5.** Thread the marinated pork cubes onto the skewers. Use about 5 to 8 pieces of pork per skewer, depending on the size and type of skewer used. Don't pack the meat too tightly. Discard any marinade remaining in the bag.

**6.** Place the kebabs onto the grill. Cook for 12 to 14 minutes, turning every 3 to 4 minutes during the cooking process. The kebabs are done once the pork reaches an internal temperature of 145°F (63°C). Remember to test for doneness away from the skewer and in several locations.

**7.** Once the pork is cooked to the desired doneness, remove the kebabs from the grill. Remove the meat from the skewers and serve in a warmed pita with tzatziki sauce, chopped onions, and sliced tomatoes.

NOTE: For a vegetarian or vegan option, use plain seitan instead of the pork and marinate for half the time listed above.

# Kansas City Pork Kebabs

MAKES 6 TO 8 KEBABS

Kansas City–style ribs are the gold standard for barbecue around the world. Unfortunately, to get them perfect requires 6 hours in a smoker, care, and patience. These kebabs start with pork butt, the preferred cut for pulled pork barbecue. Cut into small cubes, these kebabs are tender and delicious. Add in the best Kansas City Barbecue sauce, and these skewers are as close to a real barbecue flavor you can get in less than 30 minutes.

**KEBABS**

1 pork butt (about 3 pounds, or 1.5 g)
6 to 8 skewers

**SPICE RUB**

2 tablespoons (14 g) paprika
1 tablespoon (15 g) brown sugar
½ teaspoon salt
½ teaspoon onion powder
½ teaspoon black pepper
¼ teaspoon garlic powder

**KANSAS CITY BARBECUE SAUCE**

1 cup (240 g) ketchup
½ cup (120 ml) water
¼ cup (60 ml) cider vinegar
3 tablespoons (45 g) brown sugar
1 tablespoon (20 g) molasses
1½ teaspoons onion powder
1 teaspoon garlic powder
1 teaspoon black pepper
½ teaspoon celery salt
¼ teaspoon allspice
¼ teaspoon cayenne pepper

1. Place all the sauce ingredients in a medium saucepan and bring to a simmer over medium-high heat for 1 to 2 minutes, stirring often. Reduce the heat to medium-low and simmer for 5 to 6 minutes. Remove from the heat and set aside. You can double the sauce recipe and reserve half to serve with the kebabs. Simply divide the sauce in half, store one half in a separate container in the refrigerator, and then warm and serve as a table sauce.

2. Cut off any excess fat from pork roast and cut into 1¼-inch (3 cm) cubes.

3. Thread the pork cubes onto the skewers.

4. Combine all the ingredients for the spice rub and season the meat evenly. Let stand at room temperature for 15 minutes.

5. Preheat the grill for medium-high heat. When the grill is ready, oil the grill grates right before putting on the kebabs. Using long-handled tongs, dip some folded paper towels in a high smoke point cooking oil and wipe down the grill grates, making at least three good passes to create a nonstick surface.

6. Place the kebabs onto the grill. Cook for 8 minutes, turning once. Warm barbecue sauce and baste, turn the kebabs, and baste again. Do this every few minutes until the kebabs reach an internal temperature of 145°F (63°C).

7. Remove the kebabs from the grill, place onto a clean platter, and lightly tent with aluminum foil. Let the meat rest for 7 to 10 minutes and then serve.

# Vietnamese Pork Meatballs (Nem Nuong)

MAKES 4 TO 6 KEBABS

This is a popular Vietnamese dish that can be used in a soup, wrapped in softened rice paper, or served over noodles. Placing meatballs on skewers doesn't seem like the obvious choice, but it lets these delicious balls of flavor go on the grill where they are hit by intense heat and a little dose of smoke. The trick, and it is a trick, is to make sure that the pork meatballs are as dry as possible to keep them from coming apart on the grill. Cleaned and oiled cooking grates will help as well. Aside from that, these are easy and fantastic.

- 6 medium green onions, white parts only, finely chopped
- 4 cloves of garlic, minced
- 1 tablespoon (15 ml) fish sauce
- 1 tablespoon (15 ml) lemon juice
- 2 teaspoons granulated sugar
- 2 teaspoons cornstarch
- 1 teaspoon grated ginger
- ¼ teaspoon white pepper
- ⅛ teaspoon salt
- 1½ pounds (680 g) ground pork
- ⅓ cup (80 ml) vegetable oil
- 4 to 6 skewers
- 1½ tablespoons unsalted peanuts, chopped (for garnish)

**1.** Place the ground pork in a large bowl. Add the green onion, garlic, fish sauce, lemon juice, sugar, cornstarch, ginger, white pepper, and salt. Using wet hands, combine the meat with the other ingredients. Cover the bowl with plastic wrap and place into the refrigerator for 2 to 4 hours.

**2.** Preheat the grill for medium-high heat. When the grill is ready, oil the grill grates right before putting on the kebabs. Using long-handled tongs, dip some folded paper towels in a high smoke point cooking oil and wipe down the grill grates, making at least three good passes to create a nonstick surface.

**3.** Form the pork mixture into several 1- to 1¼-inch (2.5 to 3 cm) meatballs. Carefully thread the meatballs onto the skewers, making sure the meatballs adhere properly and aren't too loose.

**4.** Place the meatball kebabs onto the grill. Cook for 8 to 10 minutes, turning once or twice during cooking process. Do not turn immediately, but let the meatballs cook for at least 3 minutes before attempting to turn. This will reduce breakage.

**5.** Once the meatballs consistently reach 160°F (71°C), remove the kebabs from the grill. Some will cook faster than others. If this is the case, transfer to a cooler part of the grill or if completely cooked, remove and place onto a clean platter. Continue grilling the remaining kebabs until they reach the proper temperature. To serve, remove the meatballs from the skewers and garnish with the chopped peanuts.

# Fig and Pork Tenderloin Kebabs

MAKES 8 TO 10 KEBABS

Pork and figs work well together; however, not on the same kebab. The figs cook much faster than the pork and what results is mushy, burned up figs and undercooked pork. For this recipe, the fruit and pork are grilled on separate skewers, finally meeting on the plate after they are perfectly cooked. It is absolutely worth the effort.

**KEBABS**
2 pork tenderloins (1 to 1½ pounds, or 455 to 680 g each)
8 to 10 ripe fresh figs, halved
Olive oil
8 to 10 skewers

**MARINADE**
¼ cup (60 ml) olive oil
Juice of 1 large lemon
1 clove of garlic, minced
2 teaspoons chopped fresh rosemary
¾ teaspoon salt
¼ teaspoon black pepper

**1.** Combine all the ingredients for the marinade.

**2.** Cut the pork tenderloins into 1½-inch (4 cm) cubes.

**3.** Place the pork cubes into a resealable plastic bag. Pour the marinade over the pork and toss gently to coat. Remove any excess air from the bag, seal, and place into the refrigerator for 30 minutes to 2 hours.

**4.** Preheat the grill for medium-high heat. When the grill is ready, oil the grill grates right before putting on the kebabs.

**5.** Thread the marinated pork cubes onto the skewers. Discard any marinade remaining in the bag.

**6.** On a clean surface, halve the figs and skewer 4 or 5 per skewer. Brush the cut side with olive oil right before they go on grill.

**7.** Place the pork tenderloin kebabs onto the grill. Cook for 10 to 12 minutes, turning every 2 to 3 minutes, until they reach an internal temperature between 140 to 150°F (60 to 66°C).

**8.** Once the pork is cooked to the desired doneness, remove the kebabs from the grill and place onto a clean platter or large cutting board. Tent the kebabs the with aluminum foil and let rest for 5 to 10 minutes.

**9.** Add the fig kebabs onto the grill oiled side down. Cook for 5 to 7 minutes. Check periodically that they are not burning.

**10.** Once the figs are golden brown and softened, remove the kebabs from the grill and serve along with the pork kebabs.

> **NOTE:** For a vegetarian or vegan option, use seitan, firm tofu, or halloumi cheese instead of the pork.

# Filipino Pork Kebabs

MAKES 6 TO 8 KEBABS

Much of the flavor in meat comes from the fat, and pork butt has just the perfect proportions. Remove the excess fat only, leaving just enough behind to keep the kebabs moist and tender. This cut of pork combined with the marinade and basting sauce makes this a slightly spicy and amazingly delicious kebab.

**KEBABS**
1 pork butt (3 pounds, or 1.5 kg)
6 to 8 skewers

**MARINADE AND BASTE**
1 cup (240 g) ketchup
½ cup (120 ml) soy sauce
½ cup (120 ml) lemon-lime soda
Juice of 1 lemon
2 tablespoons (28 ml) vegetable oil
1 tablespoon (15 g) Sriracha sauce
1 tablespoon (13 g) granulated sugar
½ teaspoon salt
½ teaspoon onion powder
½ teaspoon black pepper

**1.** Combine all the ingredients for the marinade and basting sauce in a medium bowl. Divide the mixture and reserve 1 cup (225 g) of the mixture for basting. Store the basting sauce in the refrigerator in a separate container until ready to use.

**2.** Remove any excess fat from pork butt and cut into 1¼-inch (3 cm) cubes. You will need to remove some extra fat as you go.

**3.** Place the meat into a large nonmetal bowl or resealable plastic bag. Pour the marinade over the pork and toss gently to coat. Cover the bowl or seal the bag and place into the refrigerator for 12 to 24 hours.

**4.** Preheat the grill for medium-high heat. When the grill is ready, oil the grill grates right before putting on the kebabs. Using long-handled tongs, dip some folded paper towels in a high smoke point cooking oil and wipe down the grill grates, making at least three good passes to create a nonstick surface.

**5.** Thread the marinated pork cubes onto the skewers, about 5 to 8 pieces on each depending on the size of the skewer. Discard any marinade remaining in the bowl.

**6.** Place the kebabs onto the grill. Cook for 12 to 15 minutes. Turn every 3 minutes, basting with the reserved 1 cup (225 g) of basting sauce during the second half of the cook time.

**7.** Once the pork reaches an internal temperature of 145°F (63°C), remove the kebabs from the grill and serve with your favorite side dishes.

> **NOTE:** For a vegetarian or vegan option, use firm tofu or plain seitan instead of the pork. Marinate for 4 to 5 hours.

# Pork Pinchos (Spanish Pork Kebabs)

MAKES 6 TO 8 KEBABS

Pork Pinchos can be found in most tapas restaurants across Spain and across Spanish-speaking Caribbean countries. These quick-bite kebabs are also commonly served by street food vendors. It is a great small plate choice and perfect for entertaining. If you are preparing this for larger crowd, simply double or triple the recipe.

**KEBABS**
2 pork tenderloins (1 to 1½ pounds, or 455 to 680 g each)
6 to 8 skewers

**MARINADE**
¼ cup (60 ml) fresh lemon juice
¼ cup (60 ml) olive oil
2 cloves of garlic, minced
2 teaspoons ground cumin
1½ teaspoons smoked paprika
1¼ teaspoons salt
½ teaspoon dried oregano
½ teaspoon black pepper

**1.** Combine all the ingredients for the marinade.

**2.** Cut the pork tenderloins into 1¼-inch (3 cm) cubes.

**3.** Place the pork cubes into a resealable plastic bag. Use more than one bag if doubling the recipe. Pour the marinade over the pork and toss gently to coat. Remove any excess air from the bag, seal, and place into the refrigerator for 6 to 8 hours.

**4.** Preheat the grill for medium-high heat. When the grill is ready, oil the grill grates right before putting on the kebabs. Using long-handled tongs, dip some folded paper towels in a high smoke point cooking oil and wipe down the grill grates, making at least three good passes to create a nonstick surface.

**5.** Thread the marinated pork cubes onto the skewers, making sure to leave enough room in both the front and the back of the skewers. Discard any marinade remaining in the bag.

**6.** Place the pork kebabs onto the grill. Cook for 12 to 15 minutes, turning 3 to 4 times during cooking process.

**7.** Once the pork reaches an internal temperature of 145°F (63°C), remove the kebabs from the grill, place onto a clean platter, and serve.

> **NOTE:** For a vegetarian or vegan option, use firm tofu, plain seitan, or vegetables like summer squash with onions and bell peppers instead of the pork. Marinate for half the amount of time listed in the instructions.

# Pork Belly Kebabs with Plum Glaze

MAKES 6 TO 8 KEBABS

In the past few years, pork belly has really grown in popularity. What's not to like? It's basically thick cut bacon without all the sodium. However, a little goes a long way with pork belly. These kebabs make the perfect appetizer or addition to pizzas and sandwiches. The slightly sweet plum glaze caramelizes beautifully on the crisped pork belly. The trick with this recipe is a slower cook. We recommend charcoal for this one, but it works beautifully on a gas unit as well.

**KEBABS**
1 pound (455 g) pork belly
¼ teaspoon salt
¼ teaspoon black pepper
6 to 8 skewers (use a good quality metal skewer for this recipe)

**PLUM GLAZE**
½ cup (155 g) Asian plum sauce
1 tablespoon (15 ml) soy sauce
1½ teaspoons Asian chili paste
1 clove of garlic, minced

**1.** Preheat the grill for medium heat. When the grill is ready, oil the grill grates right before putting on the kebabs. Using long-handled tongs, dip some folded paper towels in a high smoke point cooking oil and wipe down the grill grates, making at least three good passes to create a nonstick surface.

**2.** Cut the pork belly into 1-inch (2.5 cm) cubes.

**3.** Thread the pork belly cubes onto the skewers and season with salt and black pepper.

**4.** Place the kebabs onto the grill. Cook for approximately 25 minutes, turning a few times during the cooking process.

**5.** Combine all the ingredients for the Plum Glaze in a bowl and begin basting during the last 10 minutes of cook time. Watch that the Plum Glaze does not burn and reduce the heat or move the kebabs to a cooler part of the grill if necessary.

**6.** Once the pork belly has a nice rosy-brown color and has crisped on the outside, remove from the grill and serve immediately.

NOTE: For a vegetarian or vegan option, we highly recommend using firm tofu instead of the pork belly.

# Cumin-Blood Orange Pork Kebabs

MAKES 8 TO 10 KEBABS

These pork kebabs are absolutely delicious. The blood oranges add a nice sweet citrus flavor and a little color. The combination of cumin and citrus works beautifully, and it really shines through in this recipe. If you can't find Pasilla peppers, use bell peppers or even Anaheim peppers for this dish.

**KEBABS**
1 pork butt (3 pounds, or 1.5 kg)
2 to 3 large Pasilla peppers
1 large sweet onion
8 to 10 skewers

**MARINADE**
Juice of 3 blood oranges
Juice of 2 large limes
¼ cup (60 ml) olive oil
3 to 4 cloves of garlic, minced
1 tablespoon (7 g) ground cumin
1½ teaspoon salt
1 teaspoon fresh thyme leaves, roughly chopped
¼ teaspoon black pepper

**1.** Combine all the ingredients for the marinade.

**2.** Cut off any excess fat from the pork and cut into 1¼-inch (3 cm) cubes.

**3.** Place the pork cubes into a large resealable plastic bag or deep plastic bowl. Pour the marinade over the pork and toss gently to coat. Seal the bag or cover the bowl and place into the refrigerator for 4 to 6 hours.

**4.** Preheat the grill for medium-high heat. When the grill is ready, oil the grill grates right before putting on the kebabs. Using long-handled tongs, dip some folded paper towels in a high smoke point cooking oil and wipe down the grill grates, making at least three good passes to create a nonstick surface.

**5.** Core and cut the Pasilla peppers into 1¼-inch (3 cm) pieces. Peel and cut the sweet onion into 1¼ (3 cm) pieces.

**6.** Thread the marinated pork cubes onto the skewers, alternating with the Pasilla pepper and onion pieces, and place onto a large parchment paper–lined baking tray. Brush the kebabs with some of the remaining marinade left in bag (or bowl) and discard the rest.

**7.** Place the kebabs onto the grill. Cook for 20 to 22 minutes, turning every few minutes.

**8.** Once the pork reaches an internal temperature between 145 to 155°F (63 to 66°C), remove the kebabs from the grill. Place the kebabs on a large clean platter, cover with foil, and let meat rest for 5 to 7 minutes before serving.

> **NOTE:** For a vegetarian or vegan option, use firm tofu instead of the pork and/or double the amount of vegetables.

# Sweet and Sour Pork Kebabs

MAKES 6 KEBABS

These fantastic kebabs can be assembled and grilled in less than an hour. If you're a fan of Chinese take-out, these kebabs will satisfy that craving. Just serve over rice or noodles for a complete meal. To turn this into a complete "bowl" meal, double the glaze recipe, divide in half, pour one half into a separate saucepan, and heat until just warm and pour over the pork and rice.

**KEBABS**
2 pork tenderloins (1 to 1½ pounds, or 455 to 680 g each)
6 skewers
½ teaspoon salt
½ teaspoon white pepper

**GLAZE**
½ cup (140 g) sweet and sour sauce
2 teaspoons tomato sauce
1 tablespoon (15 ml) sherry
1 tablespoon (15 g) brown sugar
1 teaspoon grated ginger

**1.** Mix all the ingredients for the glaze together in a small bowl. Make sure that the brown sugar and tomato paste are well incorporated. Taste the mixture and adjust the seasonings to your liking.

**2.** Cut the pork tenderloins into 1- to 1¼-inch (2.5 to 3 cm) cubes.

**3.** Preheat the grill for medium-high heat. When the grill is ready, oil the grill grates right before putting on the kebabs. Using long-handled tongs, dip some folded paper towels in a high smoke point cooking oil and wipe down the grill grates, making at least three good passes to create a nonstick surface.

**4.** Thread the pork cubes onto the skewers. Do not over pack. Season the kebabs with salt and white pepper.

**5.** Place the kebabs onto the grill. Cook for 10 to 13 minutes, turning a few times during the cooking process. Halfway through the cook time, begin basting. Do this every 2 to 3 minutes of so until the internal temperature of meat reaches 145°F (63°C). Watch that the glaze does not burn and transfer the kebabs to a cooler part of grill as needed.

**6.** Remove the kebabs from the grill and serve over rice or noodles. If you want a saucier finish, double the glaze recipe, divide it in half, pour one half into a separate sauce pan, and simmer of for 2 to 3 minutes over medium heat. Stir often. Serve the warmed sauce with the cooked kebabs.

> **NOTE:** For a vegetarian or vegan option, use firm tofu or plain seitan instead of the pork tenderloins.

# Pork Kebabs with Mustard BBQ Sauce

MAKES 6 TO 8 KEBABS

Those of you familiar with low and slow barbecue from the South will know exactly what mustard barbecue sauce is. It is often served with pulled pork, and this recipe aims to reflect that Southern USA tradition.

**KEBABS**
1 pork butt (3 pounds, or 1.5 kg)
6 to 8 skewers

**SPICE RUB**
1 tablespoon (7 g) paprika
2 teaspoons brown sugar
1 teaspoon onion powder
⅓ teaspoon salt
¼ teaspoon celery salt
¼ teaspoon allspice

**MUSTARD BARBECUE SAUCE**
¾ cup (132 g) yellow mustard
⅓ cup (80 ml) cider vinegar
¼ cup (50 g) granulated sugar
¼ cup (60 g) brown sugar
2 tablespoons (28 ml) water
2 tablespoons (28 g) butter
2 teaspoons liquid smoke
1 teaspoon soy sauce
¼ teaspoon black pepper
¼ teaspoon white pepper
¼ teaspoon cayenne pepper

**1.** Place all the ingredients for the Mustard Barbecue Sauce in a medium saucepan and bring to a medium simmer for 5 to 6 minutes. Make sure to stir often and watch that it does not burn. Remove from the heat and let cool for 15 minutes before using.

**2.** Cut the pork butt into 1¼-inch (3 cm) cubes.

**3.** Thread the pork cubes onto the skewers. Make sure not to overpack.

**4.** Combine all the ingredients for the spice rub and season the meat on all sides.

**5.** Preheat the grill for medium-high heat. When the grill is ready, oil the grill grates right before putting on the kebabs. Using long-handled tongs, dip some folded paper towels in a high smoke point cooking oil and wipe down the grill grates, making at least three good passes to create a nonstick surface.

**6.** Grill the kebabs for a total of 12 to 15 minutes. Begin basting with Mustard Barbecue Sauce halfway through the cook time.

**7.** Once the pork reaches an internal temperature of 145°F (63°C), remove the kebabs from the grill and let rest for a few minutes before serving. If using metal skewers, carefully remove the pieces of pork and serve.

> **NOTE:** For a vegetarian or vegan option, use seitan instead of the pork.

# Hawaiian SPAM and Pineapple Kebabs

MAKES 6 TO 10 KEBABS

Most people don't think of SPAM as a kebab item, but believe it or not, the sweet, sour, and salty aspects of this dish really works. This recipe is quite simple and requires little time on the grill. It's a perfect small-bite item or fast enough for a meal when you're in a pinch.

- 1 can of SPAM
- 1 pineapple
- 1 to 2 green bell peppers
- 6 to 10 skewers
- 1 cup (235 ml) pineapple juice

**1.** Preheat the grill for medium-high heat. When the grill is ready, oil the grill grates right before putting on the kebabs. Using long-handled tongs, dip some folded paper towels in a high smoke point cooking oil and wipe down the grill grates, making at least three good passes to create a nonstick surface.

**2.** Cut the SPAM into 1-inch (2.5 cm) cubes. Core and cut the bell peppers into 1-inch (2.5 cm) pieces. Peel, core, and cut the pineapple into 1-inch (2.5 cm) pieces. Thread the SPAM cubes onto the skewers, alternating with the bell pepper and pineapple pieces. Make sure to start and end with SPAM cubes.

**3.** Place the kebabs onto the grill. Cook for a total of 6 minutes. Brush often with the pineapple juice and watch that the kebabs do not burn.

**4.** Once cooked to the desired doneness, remove the kebabs from the grill and serve immediately.

> **NOTE:** For a vegetarian or vegan option, use a flavored seitan or halloumi or kasseri cheese. Obviously, these ingredients will change the flavor profile of the recipe given the salty/slightly smoky flavor of SPAM.

# Maple-Sage Pork Kebabs

MAKES 5 TO 7 KEBABS

Sweet with mild herbal notes from the sage, this is the perfect brunch or dinner kebab. It has a flavor not entirely dissimilar to a breakfast pork sausage, only several times better. Pork butt, sometimes called a Boston roast, is the ideal cut for a kebab like this. It has the right combination of meat and fat to build a moist and tender kebab. Serve with traditional brunch fare or over salads or rice.

**KEBABS**
1 pork butt (3 pounds, or 1.5 kg)
5 to 7 skewers

**MARINADE AND BASTE**
½ cup (120 ml) orange juice
¼ cup (60 ml) maple syrup
2 tablespoons (28 ml) olive oil
2 tablespoons (30 g) dark brown sugar
1¼ teaspoons chopped fresh sage leaves
½ teaspoon salt
¼ teaspoon black pepper
⅛ teaspoon cayenne pepper

**1.** Combine all the ingredients for the marinade and baste and reserve ⅓ cup (80 ml) for the basting sauce. Store the reserved portion in a separate container in the refrigerator until ready to use. Right before using, reheat for 15 to 20 seconds in microwave.

**2.** Cut the pork butt into 1- to 1¼-inch (2.5 to 3 cm) cubes, removing any excess fat.

**3.** Place the pork cubes into a resealable plastic bag. Pour the marinade over the pork and toss gently to coat. Remove any excess air from the bag, seal, and place into the refrigerator for 4 hours.

**4.** Preheat the grill for medium-high heat. When the grill is ready, oil the grill grates right before putting on the kebabs. Using long-handled tongs, dip some folded paper towels in a high smoke point cooking oil and wipe down the grill grates, making at least three good passes to create a nonstick surface.

**5.** Thread the marinated pork cubes onto the skewers. Use about 5 to 8 pieces per skewer depending on the size. Discard any marinade remaining in the bag.

**6.** Place the kebabs onto the grill. Cook for 4 minutes, turn, and baste with the warmed reserved basting sauce. Repeat the process 2 to 3 times during the cooking process. The kebabs should take 12 to 14 minutes to cook or until pork reaches an internal temperature of 145°F (63°C). Watch that the kebabs do not burn. Reduce the heat if necessary.

**7.** Once the pork reaches an internal temperature of 145°F (63°C), remove the kebabs from the grill, let rest for a few minutes, and serve.

**NOTE:** For a vegetarian or vegan option, use firm tofu instead of the pork butt.

# Bratwurst, Onion, and Bell Pepper Kebabs

MAKES 6 TO 8 LARGE KEBABS

So, you want to grill up some brats and throw them in a bun with a few onions and peppers? The problem is, and one that many people have on the grill, is that the sausages get burnt on the outside while remaining raw in the middle, cause substantial and intimidating flare-ups, and end up dried and shriveled. By cutting up these bratwursts and threading them onto skewers with onions and bell peppers, it cooks more evenly. All that is needed is to baste them with a little beer and then slide the contents of the skewer into a bun—Perfect!

**10 bratwurst**
**1 large bell pepper**
**1 medium sweet onion**
**1 cup (235 ml) beer (ale is recommended)**
**6 to 8 large skewers**
**⅓ cup (80 ml) oil**

**1.** Cut the bratwursts into 1½-inch (4 cm) pieces. Core and cut the bell pepper into 1½-inch (4 cm) pieces. Peel and cut the sweet onion into 1½-inch (4 cm) pieces.

**2.** Preheat the grill for medium-high heat. When the grill is ready, oil the grill grates right before putting on the kebabs. Using long-handled tongs, dip some folded paper towels in a high smoke point cooking oil and wipe down the grill grates, making at least three good passes to create a nonstick surface.

**3.** Thread the skewers in the following order: bratwurst, then the onion, and then the bell pepper. Repeat the process, leaving some room at the ends of the skewers.

**4.** Place the kebabs onto the grill. Cook for 3 minutes. Gently turn. If the sausages are sticking to the grill grates, give it a minute or two more and then turn. Cook for a total of 10 to 12 minutes, turning a few times during the cooking process. Baste repeatedly with beer while they cook.

**5.** Once the bratwursts reach an internal temperature of 160°F (71°C), remove the kebabs from the grill and place into sandwich buns, sliding out the skewers. These kebabs can be served as they are with your favorite side dishes or as appetizers.

# Greek Lamb Kebabs

MAKES 6 TO 8 KEBABS

Lamb is, of course, the classic meat for kebabs, and the secret here is to take all those fantastic Greek flavors and infuse them into little cubes of lamb leg. The best way to serve these kebabs is to grab a hold of the cooked meat with a warm pita and pull it off and top with a yogurt sauce and sliced onions. This is the perfect way to prepare a complete meal, quickly.

**KEBABS**
1 boneless leg of lamb (4 pounds, or 2 kg)
6 to 8 skewers

**MARINADE**
⅓ cup (80 ml) red wine vinegar
2 teaspoons salt
½ teaspoon black pepper
1 teaspoon dried oregano
½ teaspoon dried mint (or 1 teaspoon chopped fresh mint)
2 tablespoons (28 ml) olive oil
4 cloves of garlic, smashed

**FOR SERVING**
Pita bread
Sliced onions
Sliced tomatoes

**1.** In a small bowl, combine the red wine vinegar, salt, black pepper, dried oregano, and dried (or fresh) mint. Slowly whisk in the olive oil. Add the smashed garlic. Set aside for 10 minutes.

**2.** Cut away any excess fat from the lamb leg. Cut the lamb into 1¼-inch (3 cm) cubes.

**3.** Place the lamb cubes into a resealable plastic bag. Pour the marinade over the lamb and toss gently to coat. Release any air from bag, seal, and place into the refrigerator for 4 to 6 hours.

**4.** Preheat the grill for medium-high heat. When the grill is ready, oil the grill grates right before putting on the kebabs. Using long-handled tongs, dip some folded paper towels in a high smoke point cooking oil and wipe down the grill grates, making at least three good passes to create a nonstick surface.

**5.** Thread the marinated lamb cubes onto the skewers, about 5 to 8 pieces per skewer depending on the size. Don't overpack the skewer. Discard any marinade remaining in the bag.

**6.** Place the lamb kebabs onto the grill. Cook for 12 to 13 minutes, turning every few minutes.

**7.** Once cooked, remove the kebabs from the grill and let the meat rest for 5 to 6 minutes. Remove the meat from the skewers and serve on warmed pitas with yogurt sauce, sliced onions, and sliced tomatoes.

> **NOTE:** For a vegetarian or vegan option, use cubed portabella mushrooms instead of lamb.

# Lamb Shish Kebabs

MAKES 6 TO 8 KEBABS

Shish kebab is a Middle Eastern method for cooking lamb. The term *shish kebab* is the Turkish name for skewered roasted meat. The lamb is cubed, marinated for several hours, and paired with bell peppers and onions. Often, tomatoes are included, but we have found that the tomatoes cook at a much faster rate than the meat, leaving them charred on the outside and nearly liquid in the center. For this reason, we have omitted that ingredient in this recipe.

**KEBABS**

1 boneless lamb leg (2½ pounds, or 1 kg)
2 to 3 large bell peppers
1 large red onion
6 to 8 skewers

**MARINADE**

⅓ cup (80 ml) olive oil
⅓ cup (80 ml) fresh lemon juice
4 cloves of garlic, minced
2 teaspoons coarse salt
1¼ teaspoons ground cumin
1 teaspoon paprika
1 teaspoon grated ginger
½ teaspoon sumac (substitute with 1 tablespoon [15 ml] lemon juice)
½ teaspoon black pepper
¼ teaspoon allspice
¼ teaspoon dried thyme

**1.** Combine all the ingredients for the marinade. Taste for salt content and add a little more if needed.

**2.** Cut off any excess fat from the boneless leg of lamb and cut into 1¼-inch (3 cm) cubes.

**3.** Place the lamb cubes into a resealable plastic bag. Pour the marinade over the lamb and toss gently to coat. Remove any excess air from the bag, seal, and place into the refrigerator for 4 to 8 hours.

**4.** Prepare the vegetables right before taking the lamb out of the fridge. Core and cut the bell pepper into 1¼-inch (3 cm) pieces. Peel and cut the red onion into 1¼-inch (3 cm) pieces. If using bamboo skewers, soak them for 15 minutes.

**5.** Preheat the grill for medium-high heat. When the grill is ready, oil the grill grates right before putting on the kebabs.

**6.** Thread the marinated lamb cubes onto the skewers, alternating between the onion and bell pepper pieces. Make sure to leave enough room on both ends of the skewer. Discard any marinade remaining in the bag.

**7.** Place the kebabs onto the grill. Cook for 10 to 12 minutes, turning 2 to 3 times during the cooking process.

**8.** Once the lamb reaches the desired doneness, remove the kebabs from the grill. Remove the meat from the skewers and serve with warmed pita bread or over rice pilaf.

> **NOTE:** For a vegetarian or vegan option, use cremini or white mushrooms instead of the lamb.

# Spicy Lamb Skewers (Yang Rou Chuan)

MAKES 6 TO 8 KEBABS

The first time we tried these Chinese street food kebabs, we were amazed by the complexity of the flavors. There is a slow-building heat that combines with the toasted cumin that results in something remarkable. The real secret is in the toasting of the spices before it is applied to the meat. This brings out the essential oils and makes a fragrant and flavorful kebab.

**KEBABS**
1 lamb roast (2 pounds, or 900 g)
6 to 8 skewers

**SPICE RUB**
3 tablespoons (18 g) cumin seeds
1 tablespoon (5 g) black peppercorns
1 tablespoon (4 g) dried chili flakes
1 tablespoon (18 g) salt
1½ teaspoons onion powder
½ teaspoon garlic powder

**1.** In a small skillet, toast the cumin seeds and peppercorns for 1 to 2 minutes. Move the seeds around in the pan for even toasting. Once they become fragrant, remove from the heat. Place into a spice or coffee grinder on medium setting. Pulverize the seeds. Dump out into a small bowl and add the remaining ingredients for the spice rub. Set aside.

**2.** Cut the lamb roast into 1¼-inch (3 cm) cubes.

**3.** Place the lamb cubes into a large bowl. Pour the spice rub into the bowl and toss to coat all of the meat. Set aside for 15 minutes.

**4.** Preheat the grill for medium-high to high heat. When the grill is ready, oil the grill grates right before putting on the kebabs. Using long-handled tongs, dip some folded paper towels in a high smoke point cooking oil and wipe down the grill grates, making at least three good passes to create a nonstick surface.

**5.** Thread the lamb cubes onto the skewers, about 6 to 8 pieces per skewer.

**6.** Place the kebabs onto the grill. Cook for 10 to 12 minutes, turning every few minutes.

**7.** Remove the kebabs from the grill and serve. I recommend an ice cold beer to accompany these delicious kebabs.

> **NOTE:** For a vegetarian or vegan option, use plain seitan instead of the lamb.

# Pomegranate-Mint Lamb Kebabs

MAKES 6 TO 8 KEBABS

The very Middle Eastern pomegranate adds a nice sweetness but is not overpowering. The mint adds brightness to the dish. Any cut of lamb is perfect for this recipe. Look for good quality lamb, but choose the cut that has the best price. As long as it can be cut into 1-inch (2.5 cm) cubes, it will make one of the best lamb kebabs you have ever eaten. Serve over rice pilaf or on flatbread.

**KEBABS**

1 lamb roast (2 pounds, or 900 g)
6 to 8 skewers

**MARINADE**

1 medium shallot, finely chopped
¼ cup (80 g) pomegranate molasses
6 large mint leaves, chopped
2 tablespoons (28 ml) olive oil
1 tablespoon (15 ml) water
1¼ teaspoons salt
1 teaspoon ground cumin
½ teaspoon black pepper

**1.** Combine the chopped shallot, pomegranate molasses, ⅓ of the chopped mint leaves, olive oil, water, salt, cumin, and black pepper.

**2.** Trim the lamb roast of any excess fat and cut into 1-inch (2.5 cm) cubes.

**3.** Place the lamb cubes into a resealable bag. Pour the marinade over the lamb and toss gently to coat. Remove any excess air from the bag, seal, and place into the refrigerator for 6 to 8 hours.

**4.** Preheat the grill for medium-high heat. When the grill is ready, oil the grill grates right before putting on the kebabs. Using long-handled tongs, dip some folded paper towels in a high smoke point cooking oil and wipe down the grill grates, making at least three good passes to create a nonstick surface.

**5.** Thread the marinated lamb cubes onto the skewers, anywhere from 5 to 8 pieces of meat depending on the size and type of skewer. Discard any marinade remaining in the bag.

**6.** Place the kebabs onto the grill. Cook for 12 to 13 minutes, turning often. Watch that the marinade does not burn and reduce the heat if necessary.

**7.** Once the lamb reaches the desired doneness, remove the kebabs from the grill and place onto a clean platter. Let rest for 5 minutes. Top with the remaining chopped mint and serve.

**NOTE:** For a vegetarian or vegan option, use halloumi, kasseri cheese, plain seitan, or firm tofu instead of the lamb. Reduce the marinating and cooking time by half.

# Seekh Kebabs

MAKES 7 TO 8 KEBABS

Seekh kebabs are a South Asia specialty that has spread around the world through restaurants and street vendors. It is similar to koftas but uses more earthy and hotter spices. Typically, seekh kababs are served with warmed naan bread or over rice with raita (a mild yogurt sauce) and fresh greens.

**KEBABS**
2 pounds (900 g) ground lamb
¾ cup (135 g) finely chopped onion
½ cup (8 g) cilantro leaves, chopped
2 cloves of garlic, minced
Juice of 1 lime
1 teaspoon chopped ginger
1½ teaspoons salt
1 teaspoon garam masala
½ teaspoon ground coriander
½ teaspoon black pepper
¼ teaspoon cayenne pepper
7 to 8 sword skewers
¼ cup (60 ml) vegetable oil

**FOR SERVING**
Naan bread
Raita
Sliced onions
Chopped cilantro

**1.** Place the finely chopped onion into a cheesecloth or several layers of paper towel. Squeeze out all excess moisture.

**2.** Combine the onion with the ground lamb, cilantro, garlic, lime juice, ginger, salt, garam masala, coriander, black pepper, and cayenne pepper. Gently combine. Cover the bowl with plastic wrap and place in the refrigerator for 2 to 3 hours.

**3.** Form the lamb into oblong kebabs (so it looks like a large sausage) around the sword skewers. Each kebab should be about 6 to 8 inches (15 to 20 cm) long. Make sure that the meat is packed tightly around the skewer and that there is at least 1 inch (2.5 cm) of exposed metal on the end. Brush the surface with oil and return the uncooked kebabs into the refrigerator for 30 more minutes.

**4.** Preheat the grill for medium-high to high heat. When the grill is ready, oil the grill grates right before putting on the kebabs. Using long-handled tongs, dip some folded paper towels in a high smoke point cooking oil and wipe down the grill grates, making at least three good passes to create a nonstick surface.

**5.** Place the seekh kebabs onto the grill. Leave the lid up and cook one side for 6 to 7 minutes, turn, and continue cooking for an additional 6 to 7 minutes until the internal temperature of the kebabs reaches 160°F (71°C).

**6.** Once is cooked, remove the kebabs from the grill. Remove the meat from the skewers and serve on warmed naan bread with raita, sliced onion, and chopped cilantro leaves.

# Sosaties (Lamb and Apricot Kebabs)

MAKES 6 TO 10 KEBABS

This is a traditional "Braai" dish of South Africa and shows the influences of the region. There is a hint of Indian and Middle Eastern flavors in these kebabs that explain why they are a favorite. The dried apricots add a subtle fruitiness that marries well with the curry powder and a little dash of heat.

**KEBABS**

1 lamb roast (2 pounds, or 900 g)
8 ounces (225 g) dried apricots
1 onion
6 to 10 skewers

**MARINADE**

½ cup (160 g) apricot preserves
2 tablespoons (28 ml) white wine vinegar
2 tablespoons (30 g) brown sugar
2 ½ teaspoons (5 g) curry powder
2 teaspoons ground cumin
2 teaspoons salt
2 cloves of garlic, minced
1 teaspoon grated ginger
½ teaspoon ground turmeric
½ teaspoon black pepper
¼ teaspoon allspice
¼ teaspoon spicy chili powder or cayenne pepper

1. Combine all the ingredients for the marinade.

2. Cut the lamb roast into 1¼-inch (3 cm) cubes.

3. Place the lamb cubes into a resealable plastic bag. Pour the marinade over the lamb and toss gently to coat. Remove any excess air from the bag, seal, and place into the refrigerator for 4 hours.

4. Preheat the grill for medium-high heat. When the grill is ready, oil the grill grates right before putting on the kebabs. Using long-handled tongs, dip some folded paper towels in a high smoke point cooking oil and wipe down the grill grates, making at least three good passes to create a nonstick surface.

5. Peel and cut the onion into 1¼-inch (3 cm) pieces. Thread the marinated lam cubes onto the skewers, alternating apricots and onion pieces. Discard any marinade remaining in the bag.

6. Place the kebabs on the grill. Cook for 10 to 12 minutes, turning 3 to 4 times during the cooking process. The kebabs are done when the lamb reaches an internal temperature of 145°F (63°C).

7. Once cooked, remove the kebabs from the grill and serve immediately.

> NOTE: For a vegetarian or vegan option, use plain cubed seitan or firm tofu instead of the lamb. Reduce the cooking time because these options will cook much faster than lamb.

# Jalapeño, Mint, and Red Onion Lamb Kebabs

MAKES 6 TO 8 KEBABS

These mildly spiced lamb kebabs are glazed with a sweet jalapeño glaze. If you are looking to reduce the spiciness of this dish, make sure to remove the seeds from the jalapeños before threading onto the skewers. These kebabs are excellent served over rice or vegetables and as always, spicy food and ice cold beer make a great pairing.

**KEBABS**
1 lamb roast (1½ to 2 pounds, or 680 to 900 g)
6 to 8 large jalapeños
1 red onion
6 to 8 skewers
Olive oil
2½ teaspoons (15 g) salt
1 teaspoon black pepper
¼ teaspoon garlic powder

**JALAPEÑO MINT GLAZE**
½ cup (160 g) jalapeño jelly
4 to 6 mint leaves, finely chopped
2 cloves of garlic minced
2 tablespoons (28 ml) red wine vinegar
2 tablespoons (28 ml) water
½ teaspoon onion powder

**1.** Place all the ingredients for the Jalapeño Mint Glaze in a small saucepan and bring to a medium simmer. Stir constantly. Reduce the heat to low and continue stirring until the jalapeño jelly has melted through. Remove from the heat and set aside while you prepare the kebabs.

**2.** Cut the lamb roast into 1¼-inch (3 cm) cubes. Seed and cut the jalapeño peppers into fourths. Peel and cut the red onion into 1¼-inch (3 cm) pieces.

**3.** Preheat the grill for medium-high heat. When the grill is ready, oil the grill grates right before putting on the kebabs.

**4.** Thread the lamb cubes onto the skewers, alternating with the jalapeño and red onion pieces. Remember to start and end with meat when threading. Brush the kebabs with oil and season with salt, black pepper, and garlic powder on both sides.

**5.** Place the kebabs onto the grill. Cook for 2 to 3 minutes per side. Begin basting with the Jalapeño Mint Glaze after that point, turn the kebabs, and baste again. Repeat the process 3 to 4 times until the kebabs have cooked through, with a total cook time of 10 to 12 minutes. Reduce the heat on the grill if necessary.

**6.** Once the lamb is cooked to the desired doneness, remove the kebabs from the grill and let rest for 4 to 5 minutes before serving.

> NOTE: For a vegetarian or vegan option, use halloumi or kasseri cheese, firm tofu, seitan, or cremini mushrooms instead of the lamb.

# Gyro Meatball Kebabs with Feta Tzatziki Sauce

MAKES 6 TO 8 KEBABS

The Gyro (pronounced yeero) might just be Greece's most famous sandwich export. The meat for this pita wrap is typically lamb, though beef is frequently added. It is ground and formed into large cones that are cooked on vertical rotisseries. The meat is carved away in thin strips and put on flatbread with a yogurt tzatziki sauce, onions, and tomatoes. We love them. Unfortunately, they are not that accessible to the average home cook. Our solution is to use ground lamb, formed into meatballs and threaded onto a skewer. The grill gives it a touch of smoky flavor, and all you need do is pull off the cooked meatballs and place into a pita bread. *Continued on next page.*

**KEBABS**

1 pound (455 g) ground lamb
½ pound (225 g) ground beef, 90% lean
4 to 5 mint leaves, finely copped
2 cloves of garlic, minced
1 teaspoon dried oregano
1 teaspoon Worcestershire sauce
1 teaspoon salt
½ teaspoon paprika (not smoked)
½ teaspoon black pepper
½ teaspoon onion powder
Zest of 1 large lemon
6 to 8 skewers

**FETA TZATZIKI SAUCE**

1 small cucumber, peeled and grated
¾ cup (180 g) plain yogurt
½ cup (75 g) crumbled feta cheese
Juice of ½ a lemon
½ teaspoon onion powder
⅛ teaspoon salt

**FOR SERVING**

Pita bread
Sliced white onion
Sliced tomatoes

**1.** Combine both ground meats with the mint, garlic, oregano, Worcestershire sauce, salt, paprika, black pepper, onion powder, and lemon zest. Cover the bowl and place into the refrigerator for 1 to 2 hours.

**2.** While the meat is in the refrigerator, prepare the Feta Tzatziki Sauce. Peel and grate the cucumber on the large side of a box grater. Transfer to a piece of cheesecloth or a clean dish towel and wring out any excess liquid. Place into a bowl along with other ingredients for the sauce. Stir a few times to combine. Cover and place into the refrigerator until ready to use.

**3.** Preheat the grill for medium-high heat and direct grilling with the lid up. When the grill is ready, oil the grill grates right before putting on the kebabs. Using long-handled tongs, dip some folded paper towels in a high smoke point cooking oil and wipe down the grill grates, making at least three good passes to create a nonstick surface.

**4.** Form the mixture into 1½-inch (4 cm) meatballs. Thread 3 to 4 meatballs onto each skewer, leaving a small space between each meatball. Place on the hot grill. Do not turn until the lamb has well charred (not burnt) on the downward side. Once the meatballs have turned color all the way around, turn over and continue cooking to an internal temperature of 160°F (71°C).

**5.** Remove the kebabs from the grill and serve immediately. Remove the meatballs from the skewers and serve in a warmed pita bread with Feta Tzatziki Sauce, sliced white onion, and sliced tomatoes.

# CHAPTER 3
# Chicken and Turkey Kebabs

- 76 Chicken Yakitori
- 77 Chicken Tikka Kebabs
- 78 Egyptian Chicken Kebabs
- 80 Raspberry-Sriracha Glazed Chicken Wing Kebabs
- 82 Buffalo Chicken Wing Kebabs
- 83 Chicken Kalmi Kebabs
- 84 Dutch West Indian Kebabs (Boka Dushi)
- 87 Bacon-Wrapped Chicken Kebabs with Pineapple Teriyaki Sauce
- 88 Bourbon Barbecue Chicken Skewers
- 89 Chicken Caesar Salad Kebabs
- 93 Chicken Sausage and Potato Kebabs
- 94 Chinese Five-Spice Turkey Kebabs
- 95 Cranberry-Hoisin Turkey Kebabs
- 96 Jamaican Jerk Turkey Kebabs

Poultry, chicken in particular, is the most versatile meat money can buy. It works well with most rubs, marinades, and sauces and is perfect when hit with the light smokiness of the grill. We prefer chicken thighs over chicken breast because it has a better texture and flavor. There are, however, times when chicken breast is the better choice based on its milder flavor and even consistency. When using chicken breast, it is wise to brine it first. In the case of cubed chicken breast, the brining time can be as little as 30 minutes.

The best trick when using poultry for kebabs is finding a consistent cut. Turkey breast is a great choice and can be used as a substitution for most recipes. The size and shape makes it easier to cube, resulting is a well built and evenly distributed kebab. Chicken breast and thighs are a little more of a challenge, but as long as the skewer is well proportioned, it makes a good kebab.

When it comes to using thighs, don't pay extra for skinless and boneless. Thighs are easy to prepare in this way. The skin is easily pulled off and the bone cut away quickly. From here, depending on the size of the thighs, they can be cut into four or six equal pieces that have the size perfect for skewering.

Poultry must always be cooked to an internal temperature of 160°F (71°C). We often use marinades, brines, and bastes to maintain moisture and tenderness. Poultry can easily take intense heat, so cooking above this temperature is not a problem. We recommend a temperature of 175°F (79°C) for thighs to help them reach the proper texture and consistency. Be sure to test several pieces on each skewer to make certain that all meat has reached the proper temperature.

# Chicken Yakitori

MAKES 6 TO 8 KEBABS

The traditional fast food of Japan, the Yakitori stick comes hot off the grill and gets served up with a cold beer. This is a great party item that allows you easy clean up and your guests a convenient method of eating while socializing.

**KEBABS**

2 pounds (900 g) chicken breast
16 to 18 green onions, white part only
1 teaspoon cornstarch
2 tablespoons (28 ml) water
6 to 8 skewers
Oil

**MARINADE AND DIPPING SAUCE**

1 cup (235 ml) chicken broth
½ (120 ml) cup soy sauce
3 cloves of garlic, minced
3 tablespoons (29 g) granulated sugar
2 tablespoons (28 ml) dry sherry
1 tablespoon (15 ml) white vinegar
1¼ teaspoons grated ginger
½ teaspoon sesame oil

**1.** Combine all the ingredients for the marinade and dipping sauce in a medium bowl. Divide the mixture in half, using one half as the marinade and reserving the other half in a separate container in the refrigerator for use as the dipping sauce.

**2.** Cut the chicken breasts into 1-inch (2.5 cm) cubes.

**3.** Place the cubes into a resealable plastic bag. Pour in the marinade and toss gently to coat.

Remove any excess air from the bag, seal, and place into the refrigerator for 2 hours.

**4.** Cut off the top 3 to 3½ inches (7.5 to 9 cm) of the green onions. We will only be using this portion for the kebabs. Cut into thirds. Set aside or place into an airtight container and store in refrigerator until ready to use.

**5.** Preheat the grill for medium-high heat. When the grill is ready, oil the grill grates right before putting on the kebabs.

**6.** Thread the marinated chicken cubes onto the skewers, alternating with the pieces of green onion (skewered horizontally).

**7.** Place the kebabs on the grill. Cook the kebabs for 8 to 12 minutes, turning a few times during the cooking process. The kebabs are cooked through once the chicken reaches 165°F (74°C).

**8.** Remove the kebabs from the grill, place on a clean platter, and lightly cover with aluminum foil.

**9.** While the kebabs are resting, prepare the reserved dipping sauce. Place the sauce in a saucepan and simmer over medium-high heat for 3 to 5 minutes. Combine the cornstarch with the water. Add to the simmering liquid and stir gently with a whisk until thickened. Serve the kebabs with the sauce drizzled over top or on the side.

> **TIP:** When using bamboo skewers, expose only the food to the fire and shield the ends of the skewers with sheets of aluminum foil. This prevents the bamboo from burning.

# Chicken Tikka Kebabs

MAKES 6 TO 8 KEBABS

Chicken Tikka is hybrid dish that combines a dose of heat with the mellowing effect of yogurt. It was originally created to serve to British Colonialists who couldn't handle the heat of Indian cooking. These skewers are traditionally cooked in a clay oven called a Tandoor but work perfectly on your backyard grill. The yogurt marinade stays in place and creates a deep, flavor-filled crust that makes this one of the world's most popular dishes.

**KEBABS**

8 skinless, boneless chicken thighs
1 medium red onion
1 large red bell pepper
6 to 8 skewers

**MARINADE AND BASTE**

1¼ cups (290 g) plain yogurt
1¼ cups (200 g) white onion, finely chopped
Juice of 1 large lemon
2 cloves of garlic, minced
1 to 2 chili peppers, seeded and finely chopped
2 teaspoons clarified butter (ghee)
2 teaspoons ground cumin
2 teaspoons salt
1½ teaspoons ground coriander
1 teaspoon ground turmeric
1 teaspoon grated ginger
½ teaspoon black pepper

**FOR SERVING**

1 large green onion, finely chopped
¼ cup (4 g) cilantro leaves, chopped

**1.** Combine all the ingredients for the marinade and reserve 1 cup (230 g) of the mixture to use as a basting sauce. Store the basting sauce in a separate container in the refrigerator until it is time to baste the chicken.

**2.** Cut away excess fat from the chicken thighs and cut into 1- to 1¼-inch (2.5 to 3 cm) cubes.

**3.** Place the chicken cubes into a resealable plastic bag. Pour the marinade over the chicken and toss gently to coat. Remove any excess air from the bag, seal, and place into the refrigerator for 4 to 6 hours.

**4.** Preheat the grill for medium heat. When the grill is ready, oil the grill grates right before putting on the kebabs.

**5.** Peel and cut the red onion into 1¼-inch (3 cm) pieces. Core and cut the bell pepper into 1¼-inch (3 cm) pieces.

**6.** Thread the marinated chicken cubes onto the skewers, alternating with the bell pepper and red onion pieces.

**7.** Place the kabobs onto the grill. Cook for a total of 13 to 15 minutes, basting with the reserved sauce the first half of the cook time.

**8.** Once the chicken reaches an internal temperature of 165°F (74°C), remove the kebabs from the grill.

**9.** Serve the kebabs with chopped green onion and cilantro on top.

# Egyptian Chicken Kebabs

MAKES 6 KEBABS

Yogurt-based marinades work really well on drier cuts of meat like chicken breast. While Greek yogurt is delicious, it is too thick and tart for this recipe. These kebabs only need a few hours of marinating time, so they can be prepared very quickly.

**KEBABS**

3 large boneless skinless chicken breast
6 skewers

**MARINADE**

¼ cup (60 g) plain yogurt (not Greek yogurt)
Juice of 1 large lemon
4 to 6 mint leaves, finely chopped
2 cloves of garlic, minced
2 teaspoons white vinegar
1½ teaspoons curry powder
1¼ teaspoons salt
1 teaspoon onion powder
1 teaspoon mustard powder
½ teaspoon ground turmeric
½ teaspoon ground cardamom
½ teaspoon black pepper

**1.** Combine all the ingredients for the marinade.

**2.** Cut the chicken breasts into 1-inch (2.5 cm) cubes.

**3.** Place the chicken cubes in a deep plastic bowl or resealable plastic bag. Pour the marinade over the chicken and toss gently to coat. Seal the bag or cover the bowl and place into the refrigerator for 2 to 4 hours.

**4.** Preheat the grill for medium-high heat. When the grill is ready, oil the grill grates right before putting on the kebabs. Using long-handled tongs, dip some folded paper towels in a high smoke point cooking oil and wipe down the grill grates, making at least three good passes to create a nonstick surface.

**5.** Thread the marinated chicken cubes onto the skewers. Discard any marinade remaining in the bag.

**6.** Place the kabobs on the grill. Cook for 12 minutes or until the internal temperature of meat reaches 165°F (71°C). Turn the kebabs at least 4 times during the cooking process to ensure all the sides are cooked, to reduce the chance of the marinade burning, and to obtain a nice browning on the kebabs.

**7.** Remove the kebabs from the grill. Remove the meat from the skewers and serve over rice or in warmed flat bread.

> **NOTE:** For a vegetarian or vegan option, use firm tofu or medium white mushrooms instead of the chicken.

# Raspberry-Sriracha Glazed Chicken Wing Kebabs

MAKES 6 TO 8 KEBABS

For those that may not know, chicken wings are separated into two types: the drummettes and the flats. The drummettes look like little chicken legs, and the wingettes are more wing-like in appearance. Each of these cooks differently and should be divided up before threading onto skewers. This ensures proper cooking without running the risk of burning. While most people seem to favor the drummettes, the truth is, the wingette is actually better. Believe us.

**KEBABS**

½ pound (225 g) chicken wings
¼ teaspoon salt
¼ teaspoon black pepper
6 to 8 skewers

**MARINADE AND GLAZE**

½ cup (160 g) raspberry preserves
¼ cup (60 ml) soy sauce
¼ cup (60 ml) dry sherry
Juice of 1 lemon
3 tablespoons (45 g) Sriracha sauce
2 tablespoons (28 ml) water
2 cloves of garlic, minced
1 tablespoon (20 g) honey
½ teaspoon white pepper
¼ teaspoon onion powder
¼ teaspoon red food coloring
1 tablespoon (14 g) unsalted butter

**FOR SERVING**

2 green onions, chopped
1 tablespoon (8 g) toasted sesame seeds

**1.** Combine all the ingredients for the marinade, except for the butter. Divide the mixture into two equal halves. Use one half for the marinade and the other half for the glaze. To finish preparing the glaze, place into a small saucepan and bring to a quick boil. Reduce the heat to medium and simmer for 2 to 3 minutes, stirring often. Watch that it does not burn. Remove the glaze from the heat and stir in the unsalted butter. Store the glaze in an airtight container in the refrigerator until ready to use.

**2.** If you've purchased whole wings, cut off the wing tips and separate the wings into drummette and wingette portions.

**3.** Place the chicken wing pieces into a glass baking dish or resealable plastic bag. Pour the marinade over the chicken wings and toss gently to coat. Cover the dish with plastic wrap or seal the bag and place into the refrigerator for 2 to 3 hours.

**4.** Preheat the grill for a medium to medium-high heat. When the grill is ready, oil the grill grates right before putting on the kebabs. Using long-handled tongs, dip some folded paper towels in a high smoke point cooking oil and wipe down the grill grates, making at least three good passes to create a nonstick surface.

**5.** Using two skewers, thread the chicken wing pieces in a ladder formation onto the skewers, leaving a small space between each wing piece. Skewer the drummettes and wingettes separately to ensure even cooking. Discard any marinade remaining in the baking dish.

**6.** Place the skewers on the grill directly over the heat. The wings will take about 12 to 15 minutes to cook through. Both the drummettes and wingettes should be cooked to an internal temperature of 165°F (74°C). When the internal temperature reaches around 145°F (63°C), begin basting with the reserved glaze and turning the kebabs. These are best basted multiple times to layer on the flavor.

**7.** Remove the kebabs from the grill as each skewer reaches the desired doneness. Serve the wings garnished with sesame seeds and chopped green onion.

> **NOTE:** For a vegetarian or vegan option, use large pieces of tempeh or firm tofu instead of the chicken wings. Make sure to oil the grill grates well and keep a close eye on the kebabs.

# Buffalo Chicken Wing Kebabs

MAKES 16 KEBABS

These wings are wonderfully spicy but not saucy like the deep fried version that is coated in buffalo wing sauce. Instead, the wings are marinated in a vinegar and spice solution and then grilled. Be aware that the drummettes and wingettes cook at different rates.

**KEBABS**

30 to 32 chicken wings (drummettes and wingettes)
16 skewers

**MARINADE**

¼ cup (60 ml) white vinegar
¼ cup (60 ml) cider vinegar
2½ to 3 tablespoons (38 to 45 ml) hot sauce
1 tablespoon (15 ml) olive oil
3 cloves of garlic, minced
2 teaspoons mild chili powder
1½ teaspoons salt
1 teaspoon black pepper
½ teaspoon red pepper flakes (optional)

**1.** Combine all the ingredients for the marinade in a nonmetal bowl.

**2.** If you've purchased whole wings, cut off the wing tips and separate the wings into drummette and wingette portions.

**3.** Place the chicken wing pieces in a resealable plastic bag. You might need to use two bags for this recipe. If so, split the marinade in half and use accordingly. Pour the marinade over the chicken wings and toss gently to coat. Remove any excess air from the bag(s), seal, and place into the refrigerator for 6 to 12 hours.

**4.** Preheat the grill for medium-high heat. When the grill is ready, oil the grill grates right before putting on the kebabs. Using long-handled tongs, dip some folded paper towels in a high smoke point cooking oil and wipe down the grill grates, making at least three good passes to create a nonstick surface.

**5.** Thread like pieces together using two skewers per kebab. Simply run though opposite sides. This will create more stability so the kebabs aren't flopping around on the grill. Thread about 4 wing pieces onto each kebab. Discard any marinade remaining in the bag(s).

**6.** Place the kebabs onto the grill. Cook for 25 to 30 minutes, turning a few times during cooking process. Watch that they do not burn and reduce the heat if needed.

**7.** Though the recommended safe temperature for poultry is 160 to 165°F (71 to 74°C), we do recommend a temperature of 175°F (79°C) for these kebabs.

**8.** When the chicken wings are cooked to the desired doneness, remove the kebabs from the grill. Let the kebabs rest for 5 to 10 minutes and serve alone or with a blue cheese or creamy ranch dipping sauce.

# Chicken Kalmi Kebabs

MAKES 8 TO 12 KEBABS

These delicious Indian-style kebabs are reminiscent of tandoori chicken but call for toasted garbanzo flour in the marinade. If you'd like to buy this flour from a South Asian store, look for "besan" flour. It creates a nice subtle crust on the chicken as it grills. Serve with warmed naan bread and yogurt sauce, over rice with vegetables, or as an appetizer.

### KEBABS
4 large boneless, skinless chicken breasts
8 to 12 skewers
Oil
Chopped red onion (for garnish)
Chopped cilantro (for garnish)

### MARINADE
¼ cup (30 g) garbanzo flour, toasted
¾ cup (180 g) plain yogurt (not Greek yogurt)
Juice of 2 limes
2 cloves of garlic, minced
1 tablespoon (15 ml) vegetable oil
1 tablespoon (15 ml) water
1½ teaspoons garam masala
1½ teaspoons salt
1¼ teaspoons grated ginger
1 teaspoon onion powder
½ teaspoon black pepper
½ teaspoon ground turmeric
½ teaspoon ground fenugreek (substitute with curry powder)
½ teaspoon Indian chili powder (substitute with cayenne pepper)
½ teaspoon ground coriander
¼ teaspoon grated nutmeg or ground nutmeg

**1.** Heat a small skillet over medium-high heat. Add the garbanzo (besan) flour. Toast for 1 to 2 minutes, stirring often, until its pale yellow color turns to a light brown. Remove and add to a large glass or plastic bowl. Add all the remaining ingredients for the marinade and combine.

**2.** Cut the chicken breasts into 2½ x ¾-inch (6.5 x 2 cm) strips.

**3.** Add the chicken strips to the bowl with the marinade and toss gently to coat. Cover the bowl tightly with plastic wrap and place into the refrigerator for 6 to 24 hours.

**4.** Preheat the grill for medium heat. When the grill is ready, oil the grill grates right before putting on the kebabs.

**5.** Thread the marinated chicken strips onto the skewers, 3 to 5 pieces on each depending on the type of skewer being used.

**6.** Place the kabobs on the grill. Cook for 5 minutes per side or until they reach an internal temperature of 160 to 165°F (71 to 74°C).

**7.** Remove from the grill and serve. Garnish with chopped red onion and a few cilantro leaves.

---

NOTE: For a vegetarian or vegan option, use seitan or extra-firm tofu instead of the chicken. Marinate for 2 to 3 hours and reduce the cooking time by half. Watch these kebabs, particularly if using tofu, because it can burn easily and stick to the grates.

# Dutch West Indian Kebabs (Boka Dushi)

MAKES 12 TO 16 KEBABS

This is a West Indian, specifically Surinamese, version of chicken satay. Traditionally, it includes both South Asian and African elements in the recipe, which helps to differentiate it from its South East Asian counterpart. Delicious, spicy, and quick to prepare, Boka Dushi is a must-try recipe.

**KEBABS**

3 large boneless, skinless, chicken breasts
12 to 16 skewers

**MARINADE**

¼ cup (60 ml) soy sauce
Juice of 2 limes
2 to 3 cloves of garlic, minced
2 tablespoons (28 ml) vegetable oil
2 tablespoons (40 g) honey or molasses (see instructions)
1½ teaspoons grated ginger
1½ teaspoons ground cumin
½ teaspoon ground turmeric
1½ teaspoons Asian chili paste (sambal sauce)

**PEANUT DIPPING SAUCE**

½ cup (120 ml) low-sodium chicken broth
⅓ cup (87 g) smooth peanut butter
2 medium green onions, finely chopped
1 clove of garlic, minced
1½ tablespoons (25 ml) fish sauce
Juice of 1 lime
2 teaspoons honey
½ teaspoon grated ginger

1. Combine all the ingredients for the marinade. Use honey for a lighter, sweeter flavor or molasses for a deeper richer kebab.

2. Cut the chicken breasts into 1½-inch (4 cm) wide strips.

3. Place the chicken cubes into a resealable plastic bag. Pour the marinade over the chicken and toss gently to coat. Remove any excess air from the bag, seal, and place into the refrigerator for 2 to 4 hours.

4. For the Peanut Dipping Sauce, combine the peanut butter with small amounts of broth until you reach a smooth consistency. You might need to add less or more broth depending on your preference. Add the remaining ingredients and stir thoroughly. Taste and add a little salt if needed. Cover and set aside. If making this ahead, store covered in refrigerator until 30 minutes before grilling the chicken. Remove from the refrigerator and let stand at room temperature until ready to serve.

5. Preheat the grill for medium-high heat. When the grill is ready, oil the grill grates right before putting on the kebabs. Using long-handled tongs, dip some folded paper towels in a high smoke point cooking oil and wipe down the grill grates, making at least three good passes to create a nonstick surface.

6. Thread the marinated chicken strips onto the skewers in a weaving pattern. Discard any marinade remaining in the bag.

7. Place the skewers onto the grill. You might need to do this in batches. Cook the kebabs for 3 minutes per side or until internal temperature of meat reaches 165°F (74°C).

8. Remove the kebabs from the grill and promptly serve with the Peanut Dipping Sauce.

> **NOTE:** For a vegetarian or vegan option, we recommend firm tofu or seitan instead of the chicken. Do not attempt the weaving pattern, but cut into cubes instead. Marinate for only 1 hour and use vegetable broth in the dipping sauce instead of chicken broth.

# Bacon-Wrapped Chicken Kebabs with Pineapple Teriyaki Sauce

MAKES 6 TO 8 KEBABS

This is a delicious combination of savory bacon-wrapped chicken pieces that are glazed and then served with an additional helping of Pineapple Teriyaki Sauce. These kebabs make a great appetizer, but can also be served as part of a rice bowl with grilled or steamed vegetables.

**KEBABS**
1½ to 2 pounds (680 to 900 g) boneless, skinless chicken breasts
10 to 12 ounces (289 to 340 g) uncooked bacon strips
6 to 8 skewers

**PINEAPPLE TERIYAKI SAUCE**
¾ cup (175 ml) pineapple juice
½ cup (115 g) brown sugar
2 tablespoons (28 ml) soy sauce
Pinch of salt

**1.** Bring the pineapple juice, brown sugar, and soy sauce to a simmer in a saucepan over medium heat. Cook for 5 minutes, stirring often. Remove from the heat and let cool for 5 minutes. Divide the sauce in two, using one half as a basting sauce and reserving the other half in a separate container in the refrigerator to use when serving.

**2.** Cut the chicken breasts into 1-inch (2.5 cm) cubes. Cut the bacon strips into thirds. Wrap each chicken cube with a bacon slice and slide onto the skewer. Average 5 pieces per skewer.

**3.** Preheat the grill for medium-high heat. When the grill is ready, oil the grill grates right before putting on the kebabs. Using long-handled tongs, dip some folded paper towels in a high smoke point cooking oil and wipe down the grill grates, making at least three good passes to create a nonstick surface.

**4.** Place the kebabs on the grill. Cook for 10 to 12 minutes or until the chicken has reached an internal temperature of 165°F (74°C) and the bacon is cooked through. Baste with half of the Teriyaki Sauce during the second half of cooking. Watch that the sauce does not burn and reduce the heat or move kebabs to cooler part of grill if needed.

**5.** Remove from the grill. Rewarm the other half of reserved Teriyaki Sauce and serve on the side with the kebabs. You can also place some of the Teriyaki Sauce on a large clean platter, remove the bacon wrapped chicken from the skewers, and place toothpicks in each one. Nestle on top of sauce and serve as appetizers.

> **NOTE:** When making a sauce for more than one purpose (marinade, baste, or a dipping sauce), divide the sauce in half and store the second portion in the refrigerator to avoid any cross-contamination.

# Bourbon Barbecue Chicken Skewers

MAKES 6 TO 7 KEBABS

The best part of the chicken is the thigh. It has the perfect combination of flavors and meats that help keep it moist and tender. We use skinless, boneless chicken thighs in this recipe, cut into small cubes. It isn't hard to remove the skin or the bone from the thigh, so save yourself some money and do it yourself. The cubes of meat for this skewer are going to be uneven, but be patient and where necessary, roll the meat into a round before threading onto the skewer. Don't skimp on the bourbon, it is what makes the sauce jump up and be noticed.

**KEBABS**

6 large boneless, skinless chicken thighs
6 to 7 skewers

**SPICE RUB**

1 tablespoon (2 g) dried marjoram
2 teaspoons salt
2 teaspoons ground mustard
½ teaspoon ancho chili powder

**BOURBON BARBECUE SAUCE**

1½ cups (360 g) ketchup
½ cup (115 g) dark brown sugar
⅓ cup (80 ml) bourbon
2 tablespoons (28 ml) cider vinegar
2 teaspoons onion powder
1 teaspoon Worcestershire sauce
½ teaspoon garlic powder
½ teaspoon salt
½ teaspoon black pepper
¼ teaspoon ancho chili powder
1 tablespoon (14 g) unsalted butter

**1.** Place all the ingredients for the Bourbon Barbecue Sauce, except the unsalted butter, in a small saucepan and bring to a simmer. Cook for about 5 to 6 minutes, stirring often. Remove from the heat and stir in the butter. Reserve ½ cup (125) in a separate container in the refrigerator for use when serving. Set aside and let the sauce cool for 10 to 15 minutes while preparing the kebabs.

**2.** Cut the chicken thighs into 1¼-inch (3 cm) cubes.

**3.** Thread the chicken cubes onto the skewers.

**4.** Combine all the ingredient for the spice rub and season the meat evenly on both sides.

**5.** Preheat the grill for medium-high heat. When the grill is ready, oil the grill grates right before putting on the kebabs.

**6.** Place the kebabs on the grill. Cook for 12 to 14 minutes, turning a few times during the cooking process. After the first half of the cook time, begin basting with the Bourbon Barbecue Sauce. The chicken is cooked through when it reaches an internal temperature of 165°F (74°C).

**7.** Remove the kebabs from the grill and serve with the warmed reserved Bourbon Barbecue Sauce.

> **NOTE:** For a vegetarian or vegan option, firm tofu is the best substitute for the chicken thighs. Cook for half the recommended time. Serve as instructed above.

# Chicken Caesar Salad Kebabs

MAKES 6 TO 8 KEBABS

The romaine lettuce and chicken pieces are cooked on separate skewers and are assembled on the plate. The romaine will only take a minute or two to grill, so put these on right after the chicken has cooked through. Serve these kebabs as an appetizer or for lunch. *Continued on next page.*

## KEBABS

3 boneless, skinless chicken breasts
6 to 8 skewers
Oil
3 to 4 small hearts of romaine

### MARINADE

3 tablespoons (45 ml) olive oil
3 tablespoons (45 ml) fresh lemon juice
2 cloves of garlic, minced
½ teaspoon dried marjoram
½ teaspoon salt
¼ teaspoon black pepper

### FOR SERVING

1 cup (232 g) Caesar dressing
⅓ cup (27 g) shredded Parmesan cheese

**1.** Combine all the ingredients for the marinade.

**2.** Cut the chicken breasts into 1¼-inch (3 cm) cubes.

**3.** Place the chicken cubes into a resealable plastic bag. Pour the marinade over the chicken and toss gently to coat. Remove any excess air from the bag, seal, and place into the refrigerator for 2 hours.

**4.** Preheat the grill for medium-high heat. When the grill is ready, oil the grill grates right before putting on the kebabs. Using long-handled tongs, dip some folded paper towels in a high smoke point cooking oil and wipe down the grill grates, making at least three good passes to create a nonstick surface.

**5.** Wash the hearts of romaine and pat dry with paper towels. Cut in half lengthwise and carefully thread one half onto a skewer. Place onto a lined baking tray and place into the refrigerator until ready to grill.

**6.** Thread the marinated cubes onto the skewers. Discard any marinade remaining in the bag.

**7.** Place the kabobs on the grill. Cook for 10 to 12 minutes or until the internal temperature of meat reaches 165°F (74°C).

**8.** When the chicken is cooked to the desired doneness, remove the kebabs from the grill and cover with aluminum foil until ready to serve.

**9.** Clean off the grill grates. Brush the cut side of the romaine lettuce with oil. Don't overdo it; just a light coating is fine.

**10.** Place the lettuce onto the grill for 2 minutes or so or until grill marks are visible.

**11.** Once properly marked, promptly remove the lettuce from the grill. Do not overcook or the lettuce will wilt. Remove the lettuce from the skewers, top with the grilled chicken, Caesar dressing, and Parmesan cheese, and serve.

> **NOTE:** For a vegetarian or vegan option, use zucchini or any variety of summer squash instead of the chicken. Marinate for 30 minutes. Omit the Parmesan cheese and use your favorite nondairy vinaigrette for vegan diets.

# Chicken Sausage and Potato Kebabs

MAKES 6 TO 8 KEBABS

Coated in a flavorful Lemon-Herb Baste, these simple and delicious kebabs are grilled in as little as 15 minutes. Serve as an appetizer or as a whole meal. After all, these kebabs have the potato side dish built right in.

**KEBABS**
6 plain chicken sausages (bratwursts work well)
18 small red or fingerling potatoes
6 to 8 skewers

**LEMON-HERB BASTE**
Juice of 2 large lemons
8 large basil leaves, finely chopped
3 tablespoons (12 g) oregano leaves, finely chopped
2 cloves of garlic, minced
¼ teaspoon salt
¼ teaspoon black pepper
¼ teaspoon ground nutmeg (or grated nutmeg)
⅓ cup (80 ml) olive oil

**1.** Parboil the potatoes for 6 to 10 minutes, depending on the type or size. They should be slightly tender, but not mushy and overcooked.

**2.** Prepare an ice bath in a large bowl. Fill with cold water and a cup 1–2 cups of ice. Drain the potatoes and place into the ice bath to stop cooking. Let sit in the ice bath for 5 minutes. Remove and pat dry.

**3.** Preheat the grill for medium-high heat. When the grill is ready, oil the grill grates right before putting on the kebabs. Using long-handled tongs, dip some folded paper towels in a high smoke point cooking oil and wipe down the grill grates, making at least three good passes to create a nonstick surface.

**4.** Add the lemon juice, chopped herbs, minced garlic, salt, black pepper, and nutmeg to a nonmetal bowl. Emulsify the mixture by slowly whisking in the olive oil.

**5.** Cut the chicken sausages into fourths. Thread the sausage pieces and potatoes onto the kebabs, alternating between the two. Be gentle with the potatoes so they do not crack or break in half. Thoroughly brush the kebabs with the Lemon-Herb Baste on both sides.

**6.** Cook the kebabs for up to 15 minutes, basting often with the Lemon-Herb Baste.

**7.** Once the potatoes are tender and the chicken sausage is cooked through (165°F [74°C] chicken), remove the kebabs from the grill and let rest for 5 minutes before serving.

> **NOTE:** For a vegetarian or vegan option, use a vegan or vegetarian sausage. Make sure it is well made and can withstand the being on the grill. You can also omit the sausage completely and just double up on the potatoes.

# Chinese Five-Spice Turkey Kebabs

MAKES 6 TO 8 KEBABS

Turkey breast is the perfect cut of meat for kebabs. Not only is it a healthy lean meat, but it really lends itself to the grill. This flavorful Chinese-inspired marinade packs the right amount of punch into these quick and easy turkey kebabs. We've been known to make this recipe in large batches and portioning out the kebabs for weekday lunches. Serve over brown rice or with steamed vegetables.

**KEBABS**

1 skinless, boneless turkey breast (2 pounds, or 900 g)
6 to 8 skewers

**MARINADE**

¼ cup (60 ml) vegetable oil
3 tablespoons (45 ml) soy sauce
2 tablespoons (32 g) hoisin sauce
1 tablespoon (15 ml) rice wine vinegar
2 cloves of garlic, minced
2 to 3 green onions, finely chopped
2 teaspoons honey
½ teaspoon white pepper
¼ teaspoon salt
¼ teaspoon red pepper flakes

**1.** Combine all the ingredients for the marinade. Mix well and make sure the salt and honey have dissolved.

**2.** Cut the turkey breast into 1¼-inch (3 cm) cubes.

**3.** Place the turkey cubes into a resealable plastic bag. Pour the marinade over the turkey and toss gently to coat. Remove any excess air from the bag, seal, and place into the refrigerator for 2 to 4 hours.

**4.** Preheat the grill for medium heat. When the grill is ready, oil the grill grates right before putting on the kebabs. Using long-handled tongs, dip some folded paper towels in a high smoke point cooking oil and wipe down the grill grates, making at least three good passes to create a nonstick surface.

**5.** Thread the marinated turkey cubes onto the skewers, making sure not to overpack. Discard any marinade remaining in the bag.

**6.** Place the kababs on the grill. Cook for 12 to 15 minutes, turning 3 to 4 times during cooking process. The kebabs are done once the meat reaches between 170 to 175°F (77 to 79°C).

**7.** Remove the kebabs from the grill and serve.

> NOTE: For a vegetarian or vegan option, use plain tempeh, plain seitan, or firm tofu instead of the turkey.

# Cranberry-Hoisin Turkey Kebabs

MAKES 6 TO 8 KEBABS

Turkey breast is one of those meats that can dry out before it cooks through. For that reason, this recipe starts with a brine to add moisture that keeps these turkey kebabs tender. The glaze has a fantastic combination of traditional cranberry and Asian hoisin sauce. These kebabs cook fast and make a great topping for any salad.

**KEBABS**
1 turkey breast (1½ pounds, or 680 g)
Basic Brine Recipe (see page 12)
6 to 8 skewers
Oil

**CRANBERRY-HOISIN GLAZE**
1 teaspoon vegetable oil
½ cup (120 ml) pure cranberry juice
3 large green onions, white parts only, chopped
2 tablespoons (28 g) sugar
1 clove of garlic, minced
2 teaspoons sesame oil
2 teaspoons balsamic vinegar
2 teaspoons soy sauce
¼ teaspoon mild chili powder
¼ teaspoon black pepper

**1.** Combine all the ingredients for the brine in a large bowl.

**2.** Cut the turkey breast into 1¼-inch (3 cm) cubes.

**3.** Add the turkey cubes to the brine, cover the bowl, and place into the refrigerator for 1 hour.

**4.** Heat 1 teaspoon of vegetable oil in a medium saucepan. Add the chopped onions and cook for 2 minutes. Add the remaining ingredients for the glaze and bring to a heavy simmer for 2 to 3 minutes, stirring occasionally. Reduce the heat to medium-low and simmer for 6 to 8 more minutes. Remove from the heat and let cool for 10 minutes before using. You can double the glaze recipe and reserve half as a dipping sauce. If so, divide the glaze in half and store the dipping sauce portion in a separate container in the refrigerator until ready to use.

**5.** Remove the turkey cubes from the brine and place into a large strainer or colander. Quickly rinse and pat the pieces dry with a paper towel.

**6.** Preheat the grill for medium-high heat. When the grill is ready, oil the grill grates right before putting on the kebabs.

**7.** Thread the brined turkey onto the skewer, about 5 to 8 pieces on each depending on the size of the skewer.

**8.** Place the kebabs on the grill. Cook the kebabs for 4 minutes on one side, turn, baste with the glaze. Repeat this a few times during the cooking process. The kebabs are done once the turkey reaches an internal temperature of 165°F (74°C).

**9.** Remove the kebabs from the grill. Serve over rice with the reserved dipping sauce or remove the meat from the skewers and serve in a wrap or over the top of a salad.

# Jamaican Jerk Turkey Kebabs

MAKES 6 TO 8 KEBABS

These Caribbean-inspired kebabs are incredibly flavorful and versatile. This recipe calls for the turkey to be brined, so there is no need to add salt to the spice rub mixture. The Jerk seasoning has a mild heat that can be adjusted. As is, this recipe will have a hint of heat, so if you are looking for something spicy, increase the amount of cayenne pepper.

**KEBABS**

1 skinless, boneless turkey breast (2 pounds, or 900 g)
Basic Brine Recipe (see page 12)
6 to 8 skewers
2 to 3 limes
Oil

**SPICE RUB**

1½ teaspoons onion powder
1½ teaspoons granulated sugar
1 teaspoon dried thyme
1 teaspoon garlic powder
½ teaspoon cayenne pepper (add more if you want it spicy)
½ teaspoon black pepper
½ teaspoon allspice
½ teaspoon grated nutmeg
¼ teaspoon cinnamon

**1.** Cut the turkey breast into 1¼-inch cubes (3 cm) and add to the brine. Brine for 2 to 3 hours.

**2.** Preheat the grill for medium-high heat. When the grill is ready, oil the grill grates right before putting on the kebabs. Using long-handled tongs, dip some folded paper towels in a high smoke point cooking oil and wipe down the grill grates, making at least three good passes to create a nonstick surface.

**3.** Remove the turkey cubes from the brine, rinse off, and pat the pieces dry with paper towels. Thread the brined turkey cubes onto the skewers. Remember not to overcrowd the skewers. Brush the kebabs with oil.

**4.** Combine all the ingredients for the spice rub mixture and evenly season the kebabs.

**5.** Place the kababs on the grill. Cook for 10 to 12 minutes, turning 1 to 2 times during the cooking process. The kebabs are done once the meat reaches an internal temperature of 165°F (74°C).

**6.** Remove the kebabs from the grill, squeeze fresh lime juice over the top, and serve.

> **NOTE:** For a vegetarian or vegan option, use summer squash, extra-firm tofu, or plain seitan instead of the turkey. Disregard the brining instructions and add ½ teaspoon salt to the spice rub.

# CHAPTER 4
# Fish and Seafood Kebabs

- 100 Sambal Shrimp Kebabs (Sambal Udang)
- 102 Garlic-Butter Shrimp Kebabs
- 103 Citrus and Cilantro Shrimp Kebabs
- 104 Thai Coconut-Curry Shrimp Kebabs
- 106 Bacon-Wrapped Scallops Kebabs with Mint-Cilantro Pesto
- 109 Spicy Pineapple Glazed Seafood Kebabs
- 110 Honey-Dijon Salmon Kebabs with Aioli
- 111 Lemon-Rosemary Salmon Kebabs
- 112 Tuscan Halibut Kebabs with Tomato-Caper Relish
- 114 Tequila-Lime Mahi Mahi Kebabs

Fish and seafood really was meant to be grilled. The problem is that either because of the size or the delicate nature of the meat, they are a little hard to manage on the grill. By using skewers to thread smaller items like shrimp, scallops, or delicate pieces of fish, we can make this process a lot easier. It is also an option to wrap these items in bacon to both secure and flavor them as they grill. All fish and seafood items will grill very fast and should be closely watched to prevent overcooking. As always, a very clean grill grate that has been thoroughly oiled is the secret to success with all of these recipes.

When it comes to shrimp, the best way to grill these is on a skewer. By connecting several shrimp into a single unit, they can be turned efficiently. This is very important, since even large shrimp can become cooked by the grill's intense heat in a matter of minutes. The secret to making a manageable bundle is to use two skewers to thread the shrimp in an interlocking pattern. To do this, place the head end (not the tail end) into the curve of a second shrimp and thread through both. This produces a consistent skewer that will cook evenly and quickly. Cooked shrimp has a firm feel, has completely turned pink, and has an internal temperature of at least 120°F (49°C), although temperature checking shrimp isn't exactly easy.

Scallops can be handled in same way as shrimp. By using two skewers to hold together several scallops at a time, you have better control and more efficient cooking. Scallops are cooked when they are completely opaque and have become firm. Scallops are cooked at an internal temperature of 130°F (54°C). Do not waste your time grilling small shrimp or scallops. Always choose large or jumbo-sized options.

When it comes to fish, look for a firm steak cut. Fillets fall apart too easily on the grill, even if properly skewered. We prefer salmon steaks, halibut, and tuna for our fish kebabs and always look for the freshest fish possible since fish becomes mushy the longer it sits around. Fish, in general, is cooked at an internal temperature of 130°F (54°C). The flesh should be flaky, and there should be a noticeable opaqueness in color and firmness of texture.

# Sambal Shrimp Kebabs (Sambal Udang)

MAKES 4 TO 6 KEBABS

Shrimp is fantastic grilled, yet it can be a little hard to grill. Thread them onto skewers, however, and it is quick and easy. This shrimp recipe from Southeast Asia has the heat and a little sweet. For those who want it spicier, double the Sambal chili paste and it will certainly fulfill your expectations. We serve these frequently at parties as an appetizer.

**KEBABS**

1½ pounds (680 g) jumbo shrimp
4 to 6 skewers

**MARINADE AND BASTE**

¼ cup (60 ml) soy sauce
5 tablespoons (75 g) light brown sugar
3 cloves of garlic, minced
2 tablespoons (28 ml) vegetable oil
2 tablespoons (28 ml) water
2 tablespoons (30 g) Sambal chili paste
1 tablespoon (15 ml) white vinegar
2 teaspoons fish sauce
2 teaspoons tamarind paste (pulp)
1 teaspoon onion powder
1 teaspoon fresh ginger
1 teaspoon ground turmeric
1 teaspoon sesame oil (optional)
¼ teaspoon black pepper
¼ teaspoon salt

**1.** Combine all the ingredients for the marinade and reserve ⅓ cup (80 ml) in a separate container in the refrigerator to be used as a basting sauce. While the sesame oil is optional, it really does add an extra layer of flavor to dish, so if you have, do use it.

**2.** Peel and devein the shrimp. Make sure to leave the tails on. Rinse off with cold water and pat dry with paper towels.

**3.** Place the shrimp into a resealable plastic bag. Pour the marinade over the shrimp and toss gently to coat. Remove any excess air from the bag, seal, and place into the refrigerator for 30 minutes.

**4.** Preheat the grill for medium-high heat. When the grill is ready, oil the grill grates right before putting on the kebabs. Using long-handled tongs, dip some folded paper towels in a high smoke point cooking oil and wipe down the grill grates, making at least three good passes to create a nonstick surface.

**5.** Thread the marinated shrimp onto the skewers, about 5 to 6 per skewer. Discard any marinade remaining in the bag.

**6.** Place the kebabs on the grill. Cook for 4 to 8 minutes, turning 2 or 3 times. Baste frequently with the reserved basting sauce. When the shrimp is firm, but not rubbery, and the color has changed through the middle, they are cooked.

**7.** Once cooked, remove the kebabs from the grill. Serve as an appetizer or over rice.

---

**NOTE:** For a vegetarian or vegan option, try this recipe with tempeh, extra-firm tofu, vegetables like eggplant, zucchini, or hearty mushrooms.

# Garlic-Butter Shrimp Kebabs

MAKES 6 TO 8 KEBABS

If you love shrimp scampi, you will love these kebabs. Serve these as the main course or as an appetizer with a nice glass of wine. You can double the Garlic Butter Baste recipe and serve half of it as a dipping sauce.

**KEBABS**
2 to 2½ pounds (900 g to 1 kg) jumbo shrimp
6 to 8 skewers
2 lemons, cut into wedges

**GARLIC BUTTER BASTE**
⅓ cup (80 ml) melted butter
3 to 4 cloves of garlic, minced
½ teaspoon soy sauce
¼ teaspoon black pepper
¼ cup chopped flat leaf or Italian parsley
⅛ teaspoon salt

**1.** Combine all the ingredients for the Garlic Butter Baste.

**2.** Peel and devein the shrimp. Rinse off in cold water and pat dry with paper towels.

**3.** Preheat the grill for medium-high heat. When the grill is ready, oil the grill grates right before putting on the kebabs. Using long-handled tongs, dip some folded paper towels in a high smoke point cooking oil and wipe down the grill grates, making at least three good passes to create a nonstick surface.

**4.** Thread the shrimp onto the skewers, about 5 to 6 per skewer. Brush the kebabs with the Garlic Butter Baste on both sides.

**5.** Place the kebabs onto the grill. Cook for a total of 6 minutes, turning a few times during the cooking process. Continue to brush the kababs with the Garlic Butter Baste while they cook. Watch that the basting sauce does not burn and if needed, move the kebabs off to a cooler part of the grill until cooked through. The shrimp will take on a pink hue and be firm to touch when done.

**6.** Remove the kebabs from the grill, top with chopped parsley, and serve immediately.

> **NOTE:** For a vegetarian or vegan option, use mushrooms instead of the shrimp.

# Citrus and Cilantro Shrimp Kebabs

MAKES 6 TO 8 KEBABS

If you're a fan of cilantro (coriander leaves), this quick and easy shrimp kebab is for you. However, there are some folks that really don't care for cilantro. If that is the case, use Italian (flat leaf) parsley instead. This will change the flavor profile a bit, but the end result is just as delicious. Serve these kebabs as the main dish or as an appetizer.

**KEBABS**
2 pounds (900 g) jumbo shrimp
6 to 8 skewers
2 tablespoons (2 g) chopped cilantro, for garnish
Oil

**CITRUS-CILANTRO MARINADE**
Juice of 2 oranges
Juice of 2 limes
¼ cup (4 g) cilantro leaves
2 green onions, finely chopped
1 tablespoon (15 ml) vegetable oil
1 to 2 cloves of garlic, minced
¼ teaspoon salt
¼ teaspoon black pepper
Pinch of red pepper flakes

**1.** Place all the ingredients for the Citrus-Cilantro Marinade into a blender or food processor. Purée the mixture and set aside.

**2.** Peel and devein shrimp. Make sure to leave the tails on. Rinse off with cold water and pat dry with paper towels.

**3.** Add the shrimp to a resealable plastic bag. Pour the Citrus-Cilantro Marinade over the shrimp and gently toss to coat. Remove any excess air from the bag, seal, and place into the refrigerator for 15 minutes.

**4.** Preheat the grill for medium-high heat. When the grill is ready, oil the grill grates right before putting on the kebabs. Using long-handled tongs, dip some folded paper towels in a high smoke point cooking oil and wipe down the grill grates, making at least three good passes to create a nonstick surface.

**5.** Thread the marinated shrimp onto the skewers, about 5 to 6 shrimp per skewer, depending on size. Discard any marinade remaining in the bag.

**6.** Place the kebabs onto the grill. Cook for 2 to 3 minutes per side until the shrimp are firm and no longer gray.

**7.** Once cooked, remove the kebabs from the grill. Place onto a clean serving platter and garnish with chopped cilantro. Serve immediately.

# Thai Coconut-Curry Shrimp Kebabs

MAKES 6 TO 8 KEBABS

It is the mild curry flavor with the slight creaminess of the coconut milk that gives these shrimp all their greatness. While this recipe is perfect as an appetizer, the shrimp are perfect in salads or served over hot rice.

**KEBABS**
2 pounds (900 g) jumbo shrimp
6 to 8 skewers or thin sugarcane skewers

**COCONUT-CURRY MARINADE**
¾ cup (175 ml) coconut milk
Juice of 1 lime
1 tablespoon (15 ml) water
1 tablespoon (15 g) green curry paste
2 teaspoons fish sauce
1 teaspoon Asian chili paste
1 teaspoon grated ginger
1 teaspoon granulated sugar
½ teaspoon salt
½ teaspoon black pepper

**1.** Combine all the ingredients for the Coconut-Curry Marinade.

**2.** Peel and devein the shrimp. Make sure to leave the tails on. Wash with cold water and pat dry with paper towels.

**3.** Place the shrimp into a resealable plastic bag. Pour the Coconut-Curry Marinade over the shrimp. Using tongs, carefully toss the shrimp with the marinade. Remove any excess air from the bag, seal, and place into the refrigerator for 1 hour.

**4.** Preheat the grill for medium-high heat. When the grill is ready, oil the grill grates right before putting on the kebabs. Using long-handled tongs, dip some folded paper towels in a high smoke point cooking oil and wipe down the grill grates, making at least three good passes to create a nonstick surface.

**5.** Thread the shrimp onto the skewers. Place about 5 to 8 shrimp per skewer, depending on type of skewer being used. Discard any marinade remaining in the bag.

**6.** Place the kebabs on the grill. Cook for 3 to 4 minutes per side.

**7.** Remove the kebabs from the grill and serve.

> NOTE: For a vegetarian or vegan option, use firm or extra-firm tofu instead of the shrimp.

# Bacon-Wrapped Scallops Kebabs with Mint-Cilantro Pesto

MAKES 6 TO 8 KEBABS

If a recipe starts with the words "bacon-wrapped," it is going to catch some attention. The problem with bacon-wrapped foods is that seldom does the bacon cook at the same rate as whatever it is wrapped around. The trick to getting these bacon-wrapped scallops from being overcooked is to precook the bacon to a point where it is still pliable.

**KEBABS**
18 to 20 medium sized scallops
10 to 12 ounces (280 to 340 g) uncooked bacon
Vegetable oil
6 to 8 skewers

**MINT-CILANTRO PESTO**
1 cup (16 g) loosely packed cilantro leaves
1 cup (30 g) loosely pack mint leaves
¼ cup (25 g) toasted walnuts or (34 g) pine nuts
2 cloves of garlic
Juice of 1 lime
½ teaspoon salt
¼ cup (60 ml) olive oil

**1.** Place all the ingredients for the Mint-Cilantro Pesto, except for the olive oil, in a food processor. Pulse a few times to chop everything. Slowly pour in olive oil through top spout and pulse 8 to 10 more times. The mixture should have a medium-fine grind, but not be completely pureed. Let the mixture set up for 15 minutes. Remove, place into a bowl, and cover with plastic wrap.

**2.** Preheat the grill for medium-high heat. When the grill is ready, oil the grill grates right before putting on the kebabs. Using long-handled tongs, dip some folded paper towels in a high smoke point cooking oil and wipe down the grill grates, making at least three good passes to create a nonstick surface.

**3.** Cut each strip of bacon in half and place into microwave for 1 minute. Turn the bacon over and microwave for another minute. The bacon should be cooked to the point of just being pliable. Drain and let cool for 2 to 3 minutes. Pat the scallops dry with paper towels. Wrap each scallop with a ½ of a slice of bacon around the outside edge and slide onto the skewer with the meat of scallops exposed to the flame. Brush only the scallops with oil.

**4.** Place the kebabs onto the grill. Cook for 5 to 7 minutes, turning once. The scallops are done once they reach an internal temperature of 130°F (54°C).

**5.** Once cooked, remove the kebabs from the grill and serve with the Mint-Cilantro Pesto either on top of each bacon-wrapped scallop or on the side.

# Spicy Pineapple Glazed Seafood Kebabs

MAKES 6 TO 8 KEBABS

These delicious glazed kebabs call for scallops and shrimp. As a rule, scallops take just a little longer to cook than shrimp, so make sure to purchase jumbo shrimp for the recipe. That way, they will cook at the same rate, and you won't be stuck with rubbery shrimp and perfectly cooked scallops.

**KEBABS**
2 pounds (900 g) jumbo shrimp
1½ (680 g) pounds medium scallops
1 lemon, cut in half
6 to 8 skewers
Oil

**SPICY PINEAPPLE GLAZE AND DIPPING SAUCE**
¾ cup (180 g) crushed pineapple
2 tablespoons (28 ml) soy sauce
1 red chile, finely chopped
1 tablespoon (15 ml) lime juice
2 teaspoons honey
½ teaspoon white pepper

**1.** Place all the ingredients for the Spicy Pineapple Glaze into a medium saucepan and bring to a simmer. Stir often. Reduce the heat to low and let the glaze simmer for 4 minutes or so until all the ingredients are well combined. Remove from the heat and let cool for 10 minutes. Divide the glaze in half. One half will be used as a glaze, and the other half will be stored in a separate container in the refrigerator to be served as a dipping sauce with the cooked kebabs.

**2.** Peel and devein the shrimp. Make sure to leave the tails on. Rinse off with cold water and pat dry with paper towels. Squirt lemon juice over the shrimp and scallops. Let sit for 3 minutes. Move to a flat surface and pat dry with paper towels.

**3.** Preheat the grill for medium-high heat. When the grill is ready, oil the grill grates right before putting on the kebabs. Using long-handled tongs, dip some folded paper towels in a high smoke point cooking oil and wipe down the grill grates, making at least three good passes to create a nonstick surface.

**4.** Thread the shrimp and scallops onto the skewers. Brush lightly with oil.

**5.** Place the kebabs onto the grill. Turn after 1 to 2 minutes, baste with half of the Spicy Pineapple Glaze, cook for 1 to 2 minutes more, and then repeat the process. Do this about 4 times until the kebabs are done. The scallops are done once they reach an internal temperature of 130°F (54°C).

**6.** Once the shrimp and scallops are cooked through, remove the kebabs from the grill and place onto a clean platter. Briefly reheat the reserved dipping sauce and either drizzle over the kebabs or serve on the side.

# Honey-Dijon Salmon Kebabs with Aioli

MAKES 4 TO 6 KEBABS

The secret to a great salmon kebab is, of course, the salmon. Look for thick cut steaks, or better yet, talk to your local fishmonger and tell them exactly what you need. For kebabs, the salmon should be thick so that you can cut the fish into cubes. This leads to an evenly cooked fish. Also, and perhaps most importantly, make sure the cooking grates are well oiled before the kebabs hit the fire.

**KEBABS**

1 pound (455 g) salmon filet, about ¾-inch (2 cm) thick
4 to 6 skewers
3 tablespoons (45 ml) olive oil
Salt
Black pepper
½ cup (115 g) mayonnaise

**HONEY-DIJON BASTE**

3 tablespoons (60 g) honey
1 tablespoon (15 ml) olive oil
1 tablespoon (3 g) chopped chives
½ teaspoon white vinegar
¼ teaspoon salt
¼ teaspoon black pepper
¼ teaspoon onion powder
⅛ teaspoon red pepper flakes

**1.** Combine all the ingredients for the Honey-Dijon Baste. Reserve 1 tablespoon (15 g) in a separate container in the refrigerator for making an aioli for serving.

**2.** Preheat the grill for medium-high heat. When the grill is ready, oil the grill grates right before putting on the kebabs. Using long-handled tongs, dip some folded paper towels in a high smoke point cooking oil and wipe down the grill grates, making at least three good passes to create a nonstick surface.

**3.** Cut the salmon into 1¼-inch (3 cm) cubes.

**4.** Thread about 4 to 5 pieces of salmon onto each skewer. Brush each skewer with olive oil and season with salt and black pepper.

**5.** Place the kebabs on the grill. Cook on all four sides of the kebab for 8 to 12 minutes, basting frequently with the Honey-Dijon Baste.

**6.** Once the salmon is cooked, remove the kebabs from the grill and quickly put together the aioli. Combine ½ cup (115 g) of mayonnaise with the reserved 1 tablespoon (15 g) of Honey-Dijon Baste. Garnish the kebabs with additional chopped chives and serve with the aioli.

> **NOTE:** For a vegetarian or vegan option, use extra-firm tofu or plain seitan instead of the salmon. Also replace the regular mayonnaise with vegan mayonnaise.

# Lemon-Rosemary Salmon Kebabs

MAKES 6 TO 8 KEBABS

Here is an easy and delicious way to prepare salmon on the grill. These kebabs are perfect over lemon rice, on a salad, or in wraps. Be very careful turning these on the grill. As with any fish, patience is key.

**KEBABS**
1 salmon fillet (2 pounds, or 900 g)
12 to 16 cherry tomatoes
6 to 8 skewers
Oil
1 large lemon, quartered

**LEMON-ROSEMARY MARINADE**
¼ cup (60 ml) olive oil
Juice of 2 lemons and zest of 1 lemon
2 cloves of garlic, minced
2 teaspoons chopped fresh rosemary
½ teaspoon salt
¼ teaspoon white pepper

**1.** Combine all the ingredients for the Lemon-Rosemary Marinade. Remember to zest the lemon first before juicing it.

**2.** Cut the salmon into 1¼-inch (3 cm) cubes.

**3.** Place the salmon into a nonmetal bowl. Pour the Lemon-Rosemary Marinade over the fish and carefully toss to coat. Cover the bowl with plastic wrap and place into the refrigerator for 20 to 30 minutes.

**4.** Preheat the grill for medium heat. When the grill is ready, oil the grill grates right before putting on the kebabs. Using long-handled tongs, dip some folded paper towels in a high smoke point cooking oil and wipe down the grill grates, making at least three good passes to create a nonstick surface.

**5.** Wash the cherry tomatoes and pat dry with paper towels. Thread the tomatoes and marinated salmon onto the skewers, alternating between the two. Ideally, the kebab should start and end with salmon. Once skewered, brush the tomatoes with oil. Discard any marinade remaining in the bowl.

**6.** Place the kebabs onto the grill. Cook for a total of 8 to 10 minutes. Let the fish set up on the grill before turning. This usually happens after the first 3 to 4 minutes of cook time. Using a large metal spatula, carefully work underneath the kebab and gently turn. Cook for another 4 to 5 minutes or until the internal temperature of the fish reaches 145°F (63°C).

**7.** Remove the kebabs from the grill and top with a little fresh squeezed lemon juice. Serve immediately.

NOTE: For a vegetarian or vegan option, use extra-firm tofu instead of the salmon. Grill for a total of 5 minutes, turning only once.

# Tuscan Halibut Kebabs with Tomato-Caper Relish

MAKES 4 TO 6 KEBABS

You cannot go wrong with grilled fish and capers. These tender, flavorful kebabs are cooked, removed from the skewers, and topped with a fantastic Tomato-Caper Relish. Serve over rice or with lentils, quinoa, or grilled vegetables. It is a healthy, refreshing dish.

**KEBABS**
1½ pounds (680 g) halibut steaks
Olive oil
¼ teaspoon salt
¼ teaspoon black pepper
1 lemon, quartered
4 to 6 skewers

**TOMATO-CAPER RELISH**
1 cup (150 g) cherry tomatoes
4 basil leaves, finely chopped
1 teaspoon oregano leaves, finely chopped
Juice of 1 small lemon
1 tablespoon (9 g) capers
1 tablespoon (15 ml) caper brine
2 teaspoons olive oil
Salt and black pepper to taste

1. Wash, dry, and cut the cherry tomatoes into fourths. Place into a nonmetal bowl with the remaining Tomato-Caper Relish ingredients. Toss to combine, cover, and let stand at room temperature for 20 to 25 minutes.

2. Preheat the grill for medium-high heat. When the grill is ready, oil the grill grates right before putting on the kebabs. Using long-handled tongs, dip some folded paper towels in a high smoke point cooking oil and wipe down the grill grates, making at least three good passes to create a nonstick surface.

3. Cut the halibut into 1½-inch (4 cm) cubes.

4. Thread the halibut cubes onto the skewers. Brush with olive oil and season with salt and pepper.

5. Place the kebabs on the grill. Cook for 5 minutes per side or until they reach an internal temperature of 145°F (63°C). Use a large outdoor cooking spatula to assist in turning the kebabs.

6. Remove the kebabs from the grill, spritz with lemon juice, and serve with the Tomato-Caper Relish on top. You can also remove the fish from the skewers to serve.

> **NOTE:** For a vegetarian or vegan option, use seitan, halloumi, or extra-firm tofu instead of the halibut.

# Tequila-Lime Mahi Mahi Kebabs

MAKES 6 TO 8 KEBABS

Make sure to get really fresh mahi mahi for this recipe. If the fish smells overly fishy, don't buy it. We've found that sushi grade is the way to go. Ask your fishmonger for the freshest catch. Serve these tequila-and-lime marinated kebabs over rice or with steamed vegetables. These kebabs also make excellent appetizers.

**KEBABS**
1½ pounds (680 g) mahi mahi
2 cups (330 g) pineapple slices
6 to 8 skewers
Sea salt flakes
Oil

**TEQUILA-LIME MARINADE**
¼ cup (60 ml) lime juice
2 tablespoons (28 ml) tequila
2 cloves of garlic, minced
1 tablespoon (15 ml) vegetable oil
¼ teaspoon black pepper
Pinch of salt

**1.** Combine all the ingredients for the Tequila-Lime Marinade.

**2.** Cut the mahi mahi into 1½-inch (4 cm) cubes.

**3.** Place the mahi mahi into a nonmetallic bowl. Pour the marinade over the cubed fish and toss gently to coat. Cover the bowl with plastic wrap and place into refrigerator for 20 minutes.

**4.** Preheat the grill for medium-high heat. When the grill is ready, oil the grill grates right before putting on the kebabs. Using long-handled tongs, dip some folded paper towels in a high smoke point cooking oil and wipe down the grill grates, making at least three good passes to create a nonstick surface.

**5.** While we recommend using fresh pineapple, you can also use canned. However, canned slices are a bit thinner. Cut the pineapple into 1½-inch (4 cm) pieces.

**6.** Thread the marinated mahi mahi and the pineapple onto the skewers, alternating between the two. Make sure not to overcrowd the skewers. Discard any marinade remaining in the bag. Brush lightly with oil on both sides.

**7.** Place the kebabs onto the grill. Cook for 3 to 4 minutes per side or until the mahi mahi is cooked through.

**8.** Once the mahi mahi is cooked to the desired doneness, remove the kebabs from the grill, place on a clean platter, and sprinkle with sea salt flakes. Serve immediately.

# CHAPTER 5
# Vegetable and Fruit Kebabs

- 118 Summer Vegetable Kebabs
- 119 Stir-Fry Vegetable Kebabs
- 120 Mexican Corn Kebabs
- 122 Tofu, Tomato, and Sweet Chili Kebabs
- 124 Lemon-Garlic Mushroom Kebabs
- 125 Tandoori Vegetable Kebabs
- 127 Vegetable and Haloumi Kebabs
- 128 Sweet Potato and Browned Butter Kebabs with Feta
- 130 Nectarine and Basil Kebabs
- 131 Fig Kebabs with Honey and Mascarpone
- 132 Watermelon and Simple Mint Kebabs
- 135 Caribbean Pineapple Kebabs
- 136 Rum and Coconut Fruit Kebabs

There has been a long-standing effort to take vegetables off our kebabs. We are told that they cook at a different rate as the meat they accompany and will end up burnt while the meat remains undercooked. The truth is that these individuals are missing the point. We add vegetables to a kebab to enhance the meat. This is why we like to slip a slice of onion or bell pepper between cubes of steak. It flavors the meat as it cooks.

This is not to say that we should be putting big hunks of squash next to raw pork and expect it to turn out all right. There is a time to include vegetables with meat and a time to separate them. Kebabs can be vegan, vegetarian, or just a side dish. All of these are great options. We often skewer fruit or vegetables to complete a meal or to make the perfect topping for salads or other dishes. The secret with these items is the same as all kebabs. Flavor at every chance, grill hot and fast, and do all the work early.

Some vegetables are dense and will to take longer to grill. Potatoes are a perfect example. We parboil these for a few minutes before dropping them into an ice bath. This reduces the grilling time and provides a head start on the cooking process.

For fast cooking items like squash and mushrooms, we want to maximize the surface so that the grill can do its work. For example, zucchini is wonderful on the grill, but it should be pierced through the sides so that the skin can hold the skewer while the cut ends caramelize on the grill. Similarly, with mushrooms, it is best to keep the stems intact for skewering. The stems are firmer than the body of the mushroom and hold the skewer much better. To provide better control on the grill, use two skewers for each kebab to stabilize the vegetables or fruits and make turning the kebabs easier. As with vegetables, fruit should hit a hot grill for only a short amount of time.

Do not overcook fruits and vegetables. They only need the shortest trip across the grill. Grilled vegetables should still be firm, and fruit should spend just enough time to get some grill marks.

# Summer Vegetable Kebabs

MAKES 6 TO 8 KEBABS

These are quite possibly the easiest vegan/vegetarian kebabs to make. Just be sure to thread the vegetables carefully and you're good to go. The beauty of this dish is that it can be served as the main attraction, a side dish, or as an appetizer. These can also accompany meat kebabs and be placed in wraps, sandwiches, and burritos.

- 12 small cremini mushrooms, cleaned
- 1 large bell pepper
- 2 small zucchini
- 1 red onion
- 6 to 8 skewers
- Olive oil
- ½ teaspoons salt
- ½ teaspoon black pepper
- ½ teaspoon dried oregano

**1.** Clean the mushrooms with a damp cloth. Do not remove the stems. If the bottoms are a bit worn, simply take off a little of it. Do try your best to keep them intact. Core and cut the bell pepper into 1¼-inch (3 cm) pieces. Cut the zucchini into ¾-inch (2 cm) thick rounds. Peel and cut the red onion into 1¼-inch (3 cm) pieces.

**2.** Preheat the grill for medium-high heat. When the grill is ready, oil the grill grates right before putting on the kebabs. Using long-handled tongs, dip some folded paper towels in a high smoke point cooking oil and wipe down the grill grates, making at least three good passes to create a nonstick surface.

**3.** Thread the vegetables on to the skewers, alternating between each type. Brush with olive oil and season with salt, black pepper, and dried oregano. Use more seasonings if needed.

**4.** Place the kebabs onto the grill. Cook for 6 to 8 minutes, rotating the kebabs every 2 minutes.

**5.** Once the vegetables are cooked through and have some slight charring, remove the kebabs from the grill and serve.

# Stir-Fry Vegetable Kebabs

MAKES 6 TO 8 KEBABS

These veggie kebabs are a particular favorite. They can be made well in advance of any gathering and cook fast and easily, with little supervision. This is one of the quickest ways to put together a vegetable side dish that accompanies a grilled main dish. Since these kebabs are marinated, they can be prepared ahead of time and put on the grill minutes before they are served.

**KEBABS**
2 medium zucchini
10 to 12 white mushrooms
2 medium red bell peppers
1 red onion
6 to 8 skewers

**MARINADE**
⅓ cup (80 ml) soy sauce
3 tablespoons (45 g) brown sugar
2 teaspoons rice wine vinegar
2 teaspoons sesame oil
1½ teaspoons grated ginger
2 cloves of garlic, minced
½ teaspoon white pepper

1. Combine all the ingredients for the marinade.

2. Cut the zucchini into 1-inch (2.5 cm) thick rounds. Cut the mushrooms in half, leaving the stem intact. Core and cut the bell peppers into 1-inch (2.5 cm) pieces. Peel and cut the red onion into 1-inch (2.5 cm) pieces.

3. Place the vegetables into a large bowl. Pour the marinade over the vegetables and toss gently to coat. Cover the bowl and place into refrigerator for 1 hour.

4. Preheat the grill for medium-high heat. When the grill is ready, oil the grill grates right before putting on the kebabs. Using long-handled tongs, dip some folded paper towels in a high smoke point cooking oil and wipe down the grill grates, making at least three good passes to create a nonstick surface.

5. Thread the vegetables onto the skewers, alternating between each type. The zucchini should be placed onto the skewers from skin end to skin end and not through the center.

6. Place the kebabs onto the grill. Cook the kebabs for 7 to 8 minutes, turning a few times during the cooking process.

7. Remove the skewers from the grill and serve immediately.

# Mexican Corn Kebabs

MAKES 8 KEBABS

These are fantastic Mexican-style grilled ears of corn that are topped with spices and crumbled cotija cheese. It is a perfect corn kebab for any type of cookout or sporting event. By putting the corn on skewers, they are easy to get a hold of on the grill and even easier to eat.

**KEBABS**
4 ears of corn
8 skewers

**BASTE**
¼ cup melted butter
½ teaspoon ground cumin
½ teaspoon mild chili powder
⅛ teaspoon salt
Juice of 1 lime

**FOR SERVING**
⅓ cup (50 g) cotija cheese
⅓ cup (5 g) chopped cilantro leaves (coriander)

**1.** Shuck the corn and remove the silks. Cut off the pointed tops of corn (about ½ or more if it's really pointed). Cut each ear of corn in half widthwise.

**2.** Preheat the grill for medium-high heat. When the grill is ready, oil the grill grates right before putting on the kebabs. Using long-handled tongs, dip some folded paper towels in a high smoke point cooking oil and wipe down the grill grates, making at least three good passes to create a nonstick surface.

**3.** Thread one piece of cut corn per skewer.

**4.** Combine the melted butter, cumin, chili powder, salt, and lime juice in a small bowl. Brush the baste all over the corn, reserving a small amount in a separate container to brush onto the kebabs when serving.

**5.** Place the corn skewers on the grill. Cook for 6 to 8 minutes, rotating the kebabs on the grill so that the corn does not burn (or pop!).

**6.** Once the corn is cooked to the desired doneness, remove the kebabs from the grill and brush with the reserved basting sauce. Sprinkle, or roll, in cotija cheese, top with chopped cilantro, and serve.

> **NOTE:** For a vegan option, use olive oil and vegan cheese.

# Tofu, Tomato, and Sweet Chili Kebabs

MAKES 6 TO 10 KEBABS

The grilling time on this kebab is around 5 minutes, making it one of the fastest methods to make a meal you will find. Although great as an appetizer, we like to push these kebabs off onto a pile of greens for a quick and easy salad after a hot day standing over the grill. Serve over rice or quinoa for a complete meal in minutes.

**KEBABS**

1 package (10 to 14 ounces, or 280 to 390 g) extra-firm tofu
1 package (8 ounces, or 225 g) of grape tomatoes
6 to 10 skewers

**SWEET CHILI MARINADE**

¾ cup (210 g) Asian sweet chili sauce
½ cup (120 ml) pineapple juice
1 tablespoon (15 ml) soy sauce
1 teaspoon grated ginger
½ teaspoon salt

1. Combine all the ingredients for the Sweet Chili Marinade.

2. Cut the tofu into 1- to 1¼-inch (2.5 to 4 cm) cubes.

3. Place the tofu into a plastic container with a lid. Pour the Sweet Chili Marinade over the tofu. Carefully, turn the tofu pieces to make sure they are well coated. Cover the container and place into the refrigerator for 2 to 3 hours.

4. Preheat the grill for medium-high heat. When the grill is ready, oil the grill grates right before putting on the kebabs. Using long-handled tongs, dip some folded paper towels in a high smoke point cooking oil and wipe down the grill grates, making at least three good passes to create a nonstick surface.

5. Wash the grape tomatoes and pat dry with paper towels. Thread the tofu and tomatoes onto the skewers, alternating between the two.

6. Place the kebabs onto the grill. Cook for 2 to 3 minutes per side. Baste once per side.

7. Remove the kebabs from the grill. Heat the remaining marinade in microwave for 1 to 1½ minutes. Stir and either drizzle over kebabs or serve on the side as a dipping sauce.

# Lemon-Garlic Mushroom Kebabs

MAKES 6 TO 8 KEBABS

Served as a vegetarian option or a side dish, these kebabs are quick and easy and can be cooked off to one side of the grill while a main course is being cooked. The trick with skewering mushrooms is to go slow and to avoid breaking or splitting the mushrooms. Fine skewers and good-sized mushrooms also help.

**KEBABS**
12 to 15 cremini or white mushrooms
6 to 8 skewers

**LEMON-GARLIC BASTE**
3 tablespoons (42 g) butter, melted
Juice of 1 lemon
3 cloves of garlic, minced
1 teaspoon olive oil
½ teaspoon salt

**1.** Clean the mushrooms and cut in half vertically, leaving the stems still intact. Carefully slide onto the skewers, about 4 halves per skewer or 6 halves if using long skewers.

**2.** Preheat the grill for high heat. When the grill is ready, oil the grill grates right before putting on the kebabs. Using long-handled tongs, dip some folded paper towels in a high smoke point cooking oil and wipe down the grill grates, making at least three good passes to create a nonstick surface.

**3.** Combine the melted butter with lemon juice, minced garlic, olive oil, and salt.

**4.** Place the mushroom kebabs on the grill and immediately baste with the Lemon-Garlic Baste. Baste 3 or 4 times during the cooking process. The kebabs should take 6 to 7 minutes to fully cook through.

**5.** Once the mushrooms are cooked through, remove the kebabs from the grill and serve immediately.

# Tandoori Vegetable Kebabs

MAKES 6 TO 8 KEBABS

These vegetable kebabs are quite simple to prepare. Instead of sitting in a marinade, the yogurt sauce is simply brushed onto the kebabs right before and during grilling. Serve these kebabs with rice pulao (Indian rice pilaf) or in warmed naan bread.

**KEBABS**

1 large white onion
2 large green bell peppers
3 to 4 small zucchini
6 to 8 skewers

**BASTE**

¾ cup (180 g) plain whole milk yogurt
Juice of 2 limes
¼ cup (4 g) chopped cilantro
2 cloves of garlic, minced
1 teaspoon garam masala
1 teaspoon vegetable oil
1 teaspoon onion powder
1 teaspoon grated ginger
1 teaspoon salt
½ teaspoon ground cumin
½ teaspoon ground coriander
¼ teaspoon pepper flakes
¼ teaspoon black pepper

**1.** Combine all the ingredients for the baste in a medium bowl, cover, and place into the refrigerator for 30 minutes.

**2.** Peel and cut the onion into 1¼-inch (3 cm) pieces. Core and cut the bell peppers into 1¼-inch (3 cm) pieces. Cut the zucchini into ¾-inch (2 cm) thick rounds.

**3.** Preheat the grill for medium-high heat. When the grill is ready, oil the grill grates right before putting on the kebabs. Using long-handled tongs, dip some folded paper towels in a high smoke point cooking oil and wipe down the grill grates, making at least three good passes to create a nonstick surface.

**4.** Carefully thread the vegetables onto the skewers, alternating between each type. Brush the kebabs on all sides with some of the basting sauce.

**5.** Place the kebabs onto the grill. Cook for 3 minutes, turn, and brush with more baste. Do this 2 to 3 more times until the vegetables are cooked through, about 8 to 10 minutes.

**6.** Remove the kebabs from the grill, garnish with some additional chopped cilantro, and serve.

# Vegetable and Halloumi Kebabs

MAKES 6 KEBABS

Halloumi is a delicious, hearty Middle Eastern cheese that blooms in flavor once it's cooked. This recipe is simple and perfect for the kebab novice.

**1 package (8 ounces, or 225 g) halloumi cheese**
**2 small zucchini**
**1 red onion**
**6 skewers**
**¼ teaspoon salt**
**¼ teaspoon black pepper**
**Olive oil**

**1.** Cut the halloumi cheese into 1¾-inch (4.5 cm) cubes (rectangles). Cut the zucchini into ¾-inch (2 cm) rounds. Peel and cut the red onion into 1¾-inch (4.5 cm) pieces.

**2.** Preheat the grill for medium-high heat. When the grill is ready, oil the grill grates right before putting on the kebabs. Using long-handled tongs, dip some folded paper towels in a high smoke point cooking oil and wipe down the grill grates, making at least three good passes to create a nonstick surface.

**3.** Thread the halloumi onto the skewers, alternating with the zucchini and red onion pieces. Make sure that the cut sides face downward, so that a larger surface area will hit the grill. Brush the kebabs with olive oil on both sides and season well with salt and black pepper.

**4.** Place the kebabs on the grill. Cook for a total of 7 to 8 minutes, turning once or twice during cooking process.

**5.** Remove the kebabs from the grill and serve.

**NOTE:** For a vegan option, use extra-firm tofu instead of the halloumi cheese.

# Sweet Potato and Browned Butter Kebabs with Feta

MAKES 4 TO 6 KEBABS

Are you looking for a side dish to those steak kebabs? Try a couple of sticks of grilled sweet potato, basted in browned butter, and topped with almonds and feta cheese (or try toasted pine nuts and blue cheese for variation). These are so good, you just might forget about the steak.

**KEBABS**
2 large sweet potatoes
2 teaspoons salt
4 to 6 skewers

**BROWNED BUTTER SAUCE**
⅓ cup (75 ml) butter

**FOR SERVING**
¼ cup (25 g) toasted almonds, chopped
¼ cup (38 ml) crumbled feta
Chopped chives

**1.** Place the butter in a saucepan over medium-low heat until milk solids begin to surface. The butter will turn a brownish color. Remove from the heat. Set a clean cheesecloth or folded paper towel into a strainer. Strain the browned butter through. Set aside.

**2.** Bring 8 cups (2 L) of water to a boil. Cut the sweet potatoes into 1-inch (2.5 cm) thick rounds, leaving the skin on. Add the salt and the sweet potato rounds to the boiling water. Parboil for 10 minutes.

**3.** Fill a large bowl with cold water and ice. Drain the potatoes into a colander and immerse into ice bath for 10 to 15 minutes. Drain once more and pat the pieces dry with paper towels. Cut into halves (if using thinner sweet potato) or quarters (for a thicker sweet potato).

**4.** Preheat the grill for medium-high heat. When the grill is ready, oil the grill grates right before putting on the kebabs. Using long-handled tongs, dip some folded paper towels in a high smoke point cooking oil and wipe down the grill grates, making at least three good passes to create a nonstick surface.

**5.** Remove the skins from the sweet potato rounds and carefully thread onto the skewers. Brush both sides of the kebabs with some of the Browned Butter Sauce.

**6.** Place the kebabs onto the grill. Cook for 4 minutes per side or until sweet potatoes are tender and have decent grill markings.

**7.** Remove the kebabs from the grill. Carefully remove the sweet potatoes from the skewers. Arrange on a serving platter. Drizzle with the remaining Browned Butter Sauce and top with chopped almonds, crumbled feta, and chopped chives. Serve immediately.

# Nectarine and Basil Kebabs

MAKES 6 TO 8 KEBABS

Believe it or not, basil and nectarines actually work very well together. For this recipe, the basil is included in a sauce that accompanies the kebabs. We recommend serving this dish with a nice scoop of vanilla or coconut ice cream.

**KEBABS**
6 to 8 large ripe nectarines
6 to 8 skewers
Oil

**BASIL SAUCE**
¾ cup (240 g) apricot preserves
2 tablespoons (28 ml) white rum
3 basil leaves, bruised

**1.** Place the apricot preserves, rum, and bruised basil leaves into a saucepan. Heat over medium-low heat until all ingredients have melted through. Make sure to stir and watch that it does not burn. Remove from the heat, cover, and keep warm. Right before serving, remove the basil leaves.

**2.** Preheat the grill for medium-high heat. When the grill is ready, oil the grill grates right before putting on the kebabs. Using long-handled tongs, dip some folded paper towels in a high smoke point cooking oil and wipe down the grill grates, making at least three good passes to create a nonstick surface.

**3.** Wash, dry off, and cut the nectarines in half. Remove the pits and cut each half into half again.

**4.** Thread the slices onto the skewers. If the slices are too large and awkward to work with, either cut them into smaller pieces or use two skewers to stabilize the pieces. Lightly brush the nectarines with oil.

**5.** Place the kebabs onto the grill. Cook the kebabs for 1 to 2 minutes per side until grill marks form.

**6.** Once the nectarines are properly marked, remove the kebabs from the grill. Carefully remove the grilled nectarines from the skewers. Place into individual serving dishes with a scoop of ice cream on top and a spoonful or two of the Basil Sauce.

> **NOTE:** For a vegan option, top with whipped coconut cream.

# Fig Kebabs with Honey and Mascarpone

MAKES 4 TO 6 KEBABS

This is one of those Old World dishes that uses simple ingredients and produces a delicious outcome. If you are interested in Mediterranean foods, these kebabs might just be the dessert you're looking for. We suggest using agave syrup and whipped coconut cream for a vegan alternative.

**KEBABS**
1½ pounds (680 g) fresh figs
4 to 6 skewers
Oil

**FOR SERVING**
1 cup (240 g) mascarpone cheese
⅓ cup (115 g) good quality honey

**1.** Preheat the grill for medium-high heat. When the grill is ready, oil the grill grates right before putting on the kebabs. Using long-handled tongs, dip some folded paper towels in a high smoke point cooking oil and wipe down the grill grates, making at least three good passes to create a nonstick surface.

**2.** Gently rinse off figs and dry with a clean kitchen cloth or paper towel. Cut each fig in half lengthwise. Carefully thread about 4 to 5 pieces onto each skewer. Lightly brush both sides of the figs with a neutral-flavored oil.

**3.** Place the kebabs onto the grill, cut-side down. Cook for 2 to 3 minutes. Gently turn and grill for another 1 to 2 minutes.

**4.** Once the figs are cooked to the desired doneness, promptly remove the kebabs from the grill and plate. Either serve on skewers or remove the figs and place into bowls with a spoonful of mascarpone cheese and a little honey.

> **TIP:** You can use flavored honey in this dish if you'd like. Lavender honey is always a good choice.

# Watermelon and Simple Mint Syrup Kebabs

MAKES 6 TO 10 KEBABS

These watermelon kebabs are grilled hot and fast and then drizzled with a light mint syrup and garnished with fresh mint. They are a refreshing and delicious addition for summer cookouts.

**KEBABS**
1 medium ripe, seedless watermelon
6 to 10 skewers
6 large mint leaves, finely chopped (for garnish)

**SIMPLE MINT SYRUP**
1 cup (235 ml) water (lukewarm)
1 cup (200 g) granulated sugar
3 large mint leaves, bruised
Pinch of salt

**1.** In a small saucepan, bring the water and sugar to a simmer. Make sure to stir often. After a minute or two, add the mint leaves and a pinch of salt. The syrup will set up quickly, so once it reaches the consistency of melted honey, remove from the heat. Any longer and the syrup will begin to crystallize. Remove the mint leaves, cover the pan, and keep the syrup warm.

**2.** Preheat the grill for high heat. When the grill is ready, oil the grill grates right before putting on the kebabs. Using long-handled tongs, dip some folded paper towels in a high smoke point cooking oil and wipe down the grill grates, making at least three good passes to create a nonstick surface.

**3.** Cut the watermelon into 2-inch (5 cm) cubes.

**4.** Thread the watermelon pieces onto the skewers. Be very gentle so the watermelon doesn't break.

**5.** Place the kebabs onto the grill. Cook all four sides for 30 to 35 seconds. The object is to get grill marks, not to cook the watermelon through.

**6.** Once the watermelon is properly marked, promptly remove the kebabs from the grill and place onto a serving platter. Drizzle with the Simple Mint Syrup and garnish with chopped mint. Serve immediately.

# Caribbean Pineapple Kebabs

MAKES 4 TO 6 KEBABS

This is a simple recipe for a delicious, juicy, rum and brown sugar–rubbed pineapple kebab. Serve these hot off the grill with a scoop of vanilla ice cream. It's perfect for summer evenings and casual gatherings.

**KEBABS**
1 large pineapple
4 to 6 skewers

**BASTE**
½ cup (115 g) packed brown sugar (we recommend dark)
¼ cup (60 ml) melted unsalted butter
1 shot of dark rum

**1.** Cut the ends off of pineapple. Stand it upright and using a sharp knife, make cutting movements from the top downward, removing the outer peel and pineapple "eyes." Cut off the stem and cut through the center vertically and cut the half into halves. Cut away the core of the pineapple by making one straight cut downward at the pointed edge. Cut the pineapple into uniform 2-inch (5 cm) cubes. Carefully thread onto the skewers.

**2.** Preheat the grill for medium heat. When the grill is ready, oil the grill grates right before putting on the kebabs. Using long-handled tongs, dip some folded paper towels in a high smoke point cooking oil and wipe down the grill grates, making at least three good passes to create a nonstick surface.

**3.** Combine the brown sugar with the melted butter and dark rum. Stir thoroughly until the brown sugar begins to dissolve.

**4.** Place the pineapple kebabs on the grill and brush with the brown sugar mixture. After a minute or two, turn and brush with the mixture again. Baste two more times until the kebabs have grill marks and are well coated in basting sauce.

**5.** Once the pineapple is properly marked and coated in basting sauce, remove the kebabs from the grill and serve.

> **NOTE:** For a vegan option, serve the kebabs with whipped coconut cream.

# Rum and Coconut Fruit Kebabs

MAKES 6 TO 8 KEBABS

This is another delicious Caribbean-inspired fruit kebab. Make sure you have a good rum for this recipe. Nothing will spoil this dish like a low-quality, bitter rum. If you cannot find mangoes, you can substitute with papaya. Just make sure it is firm and not overly ripe.

**KEBABS**
1 pineapple
2 large firm mangoes (ripe but not mushy)
3 to 4 yellow bananas (again, not overly ripe)
6 to 8 skewers
Oil
¼ cup (15 g) toasted coconut flakes, for garnish

**RUM SAUCE**
½ cup (115 g) brown sugar
¼ cup (60 ml) dark rum
¼ teaspoon cinnamon
¼ teaspoon ground nutmeg
¼ teaspoon allspice
Pinch of salt

**1.** Simmer all the ingredients for the Rum Sauce over medium heat. Stir often. Reduce the heat to low and simmer for 1 to 2 minutes more until the brown sugar is no longer gritty. Remove from the heat, cover, and keep warm.

**2.** Prepare the fruit. Peel, core, and cut pineapple into 2-inch (5 cm) pieces. Cut the mangoes into 1½-inch (4 in) pieces. Cut the bananas into 2-inch (5 cm) pieces.

**3.** Preheat the grill for medium-high heat. When the grill is ready, oil the grill grates right before putting on the kebabs. Using long-handled tongs, dip some folded paper towels in a high smoke point cooking oil and wipe down the grill grates, making at least three good passes to create a nonstick surface.

**4.** Thread the fruit onto the skewers, alternating between each type. Do not overcrowd. Brush lightly with a neutral-flavored oil.

**5.** Place the kebabs onto the grill. Cook the kebabs for 2 minutes per side. The object is to get some good grill marks on the fruit, not to cook it through.

**6.** Once the fruit is properly marked, promptly remove the kebabs from the grill and place onto a platter. Drizzle with warm Rum Sauce, garnish the kebabs with toasted coconut flakes, and serve.

> **TIP:** To toast the coconut flakes, spread the instructed amount onto a baking sheet. Bake at 350°F (180°C, or gas mark 4) until golden brown. This will take about 4 to 5 minutes. Remove from the oven and let cool for 5 minutes before using.

# About the Authors

DERRICK RICHES has served as the Barbecue & Grilling expert at About.com for the last two decades. As one of the most popular destinations for outdoor cooking information, he has answered thousands of questions, written hundreds of articles, and explored barbecue in its widest definition. During this time he has traveled the world, grilled on almost every conceivably kind of cooking equipment and judged the best barbecue in the world.

SABRINA BAKSH is a recipe developer, editor, food stylist, and food photographer whose work has been published in a variety of online and print venues. She has traveled the world exploring flavors, cultures, and food history.

# Acknowledgments

A kebab is nothing without someone to try it. We would like to thank our friends and families for stepping up to sample our experiments, successful or not and for providing feedback on all the recipes that appear in this book. They helped us find out which dishes were too spicy, not spicy enough, which ones worked and which ones fell flat.

Dan Rosenberg of Harvard Common Press provided the opportunity to write this book, kept the ideas coming, and guided us through to the end. John Gettings' masterful eye made these pages beautiful and everyone at Quarto Publishing guided us with paperwork, signed checks, and made this book possible.

Will Wilson at Snider Bros Meats patiently dug through meat cases and the back room to find perfect cuts, and offered invaluable advice that only a great butcher can. The innumerable manufacturers, inventors, and suppliers who have filled out patio, garage, and basement with test products, prototypes, and demonstration units over the years making this job so much easier and allowing us to test these recipes on every conceivable style and type of grill.

And thanks are endlessly owed to the legions of readers over the years whose questions and comments have challenged everything we ever thought we knew about outdoor cooking.

# Index

Aioli, Honey-Dijon Salmon Kebabs with, 110
Aji Panca paste, 24
Apricots
    Lamb and Apricot Kebabs, 69
    Nectarine and Basil Kebabs, 130
Avocado oil, 16

Bacon, used with fish and seafood, 99
Bacon-Wrapped Chicken Kebabs with Pineapple Teriyaki Sauce, 87
Bacon-Wrapped Scallops Kebabs with Mint-Cilantro Pesto, 106
Balsamic-Brown Sugar Steak and Onion Kebabs, 22
Bamboo skewers, 8, 15
Bananas, 136
Barbecue sauce
    Bourbon Barbecue Chicken Skewers, 88
    Citrus-Horseradish Beef Kebabs, 28
    Kansas City Barbecue Sauce, 44
    Pork Kebabs with Mustard BBQ Sauce, 56
Basic Brine Recipe, 12, 95, 96
Basil Sauce, 130
Bastes, 12. *See also* Sauces
    Balsamic-Brown Sugar Steak and Onion Kebabs, 22
    Caribbean Pineapple Kebabs, 135
    Chicken Tikka Kebabs, 77
    Citrus-Horseradish Beef Kebabs, 28
    Filipino Pork Kebabs, 50
    Garlic Butter, 102
    Honey-Dijon, 110
    Lemon-Garlic, 124
    Lemon-Herb, 93
    Maple-Sage Pork Kebabs, 59
    Mexican Corn Kebabs, 120
    Sambal Shrimp Kebabs, 101
    Tandoori Vegetable Kebabs, 125
Basting brush, 12
Beef. *See also* Beef sirloin; Boneless beef short ribs; Chuck roast; Ground beef
    favorite cuts for kebabs, 19
    mushrooms as alternative to, 13
    overcooking, 19
Beef Fajita Kebabs, 32
Beef heart, 24
Beef loin, 19
Beef Satay with Peanut Sauce, 38–39
Beef sirloin
    Citrus-Horseradish Beef Kebabs, 28
    Harissa Beef Kebabs, 30
    Lebanese Beef Kofta, 20
    Steak and Potato Kebabs, 27
    Steakhouse Kebabs, 36–37
Beef Teriyaki Kebabs, 34–35
Beer
    Beef Fajita Kebabs, 32
    Bratwurst, Onion, and Bell Pepper Kebabs, 61
Bell peppers, 15
    Beef Teriyaki Kebabs, 34–35
    Bratwurst, Onion, and Bell Pepper Kebabs, 61
    Chicken Tikka Kebabs, 77
    Harissa Beef Kebabs, 30
    Hawaiian SPAM and Pineapple Kebabs, 58
    Lamb Shish Kebabs, 63
    Stir-Fry Vegetable Kebabs, 119
    Summer Vegetable Kebabs, 118
    Tandoori Vegetable Kebabs, 125
Besan flour, 83
Boka Dushi (Dutch West Indian Kebabs), 84–85
Boneless beef short ribs
    Beef Teriyaki Kebabs, 34–35
    Chipotle-Adobo Beef Kebabs, 41
    Peruvian Anticuchos, 24
    Sesame Beef Kebabs, 37
    Steak and Mushroom Kebabs, 29
Boston roast, 44. *See also* Pork butt
Bourbon Barbecue Chicken Skewers, 88
Bourbon Barbecue Sauce, 88
Bratwurst, Onion, and Bell Pepper Kebabs, 60, 61
Brines, 12, 75, 95, 96
Browned Butter Sauce, 128
Buffalo Chicken Wing Kebabs, 82
Butchers, meat cut by, 14, 19

Canola oil, 16
Caribbean Pineapple Kebabs, 135
Carne Asada Kebabs, 25
Charcoal grills, 17
Cheeses, 13. *See also* Feta cheese; Parmesan cheese
    Fig Kebabs with Honey and Mascarpone, 131
    Mexican Corn Kebabs, 120
    Vegetable and Halloumi Kebabs, 127
Cherry tomatoes, 111, 112
Chicken breast, 75
    Bacon-Wrapped Chicken Kebabs with Pineapple Teriyaki Sauce, 87
    Chicken Kalmi Kebabs, 83
    Chicken Yakitori, 76
    cubing, 14
    Dutch West Indian Kebabs, 84
    Egyptian Chicken Kebabs, 78
Chicken Caesar Salad Kebabs, 89–90
Chicken Kalmi Kebabs, 83
Chicken Sausage and Potato Kebabs, 93
Chicken thighs, 75, 77, 88
Chicken Tikka Kebabs, 77
Chicken wings
    Buffalo Chicken Wing Kebabs, 82
    Raspberry-Sriracha Glazed Chicken Wing Kebabs, 80–81
    two types of, 80

Chicken Yakitori, 76
Chinese Five Spice Turkey Kebabs, 94
Chipotle-Adobe Beef Kebabs, 41
Chuck roast, 19
    Balsamic-Brown Sugar Steak and Onion Kebabs, 22
    Beef Fajita Kebabs, 32
    Peruvian Anticuchos, 24
Cilantro
    Citrus and Cilantro Shrimp Kebabs, 103
    Mexican Corn Kebabs, 120
    Mint-Cilantro Pesto, 106
    Tandoori Vegetable Kebab baste, 125
Citrus and Cilantro Shrimp Kebabs, 103
Citrus-Horseradish Beef Kebabs, 28
Coconut-Curry Marinade, 104
Coconut flakes, 136
Coconut milk, 103
Cooking temperatures
    beef, 19
    fish and seafood, 99
    lamb, 43
    pork, 43
    poultry, 75
Corn, Mexican Corn Kebabs, 120
Cotija cheese, 120
Cranberry-Hoisin Glaze, 95
Cranberry-Hoisin Turkey Kebabs, 95
Cremini mushrooms, 13, 63, 118, 124
Cubes of meat, threading, 13–14
Cumin-Blood Orange Pork Kebabs, 54
Cuts of beef, 19
Cuts of fish, 99
Cuts of lamb, 43
Cuts of pork, 43
Cutting vegetables, 15

Dipping sauces
    Balsamic-Brown Sugar Steak and Onion Kebabs, 22
    Chicken Yakitori, 76

Cranberry-Hoisin Turkey Kebabs, 95
Garlic Butter Baste as a, 102
    Peanut, 84–85
    Spicy Pineapple, 109
Drummettes, 80–81, 82
Dutch West Indian Kebabs (Boka Dushi), 84

Egyptian Chicken Kebabs, 78
Electric grills, 17

Fajita kebabs, beef, 32
Fat to lean ratio
    in beef, 19, 34
    in lamb, 43
    in pork, 43
Feta cheese, 72, 128
Feta Tzatziki Sauce, 72
Fig and Pork Tenderloin Kebabs, 49
Fig Kebabs with Honey and Mascarpone, 131
Filipino Pork Kebabs, 50
Fire Wire, 10
Fish. *See also* Salmon filet
    cooking temperature, 99
    cut of, 99
    grilling, 99
    Tequila-Lime Mahi Mahi Kebabs, 114
    Tuscan Halibut Kebabs, 112
Flat iron steak, West African Beef Kebabs, 33
Flats (chicken wings), 80
Flexible skewers, 10
Fruit
    Caribbean Pineapple Kebabs, 135
    Fig Kebabs with Honey and Mascarpone, 131
    Nectarine and Basil Kebabs, 130
    Rum and Coconut Fruit Kebabs, 136
    Watermelon and Simple Mint Syrup Kebabs, 132

Garam masala, 66, 83, 125
Garbanzo flour, 83
Garlic-Butter Shrimp Kebabs, 102
Gas grills, 17
Glazes
    Cranberry-Hoisin Glaze, 95
    Jalapeño Mint, 70
    Plum Glaze, 52
    Raspberry-Sriracha, 80
    Spicy Pineapple, 109
    for Sweet and Sour Pork Kebabs, 55
Gloves, heat-resistant, 16
Grapeseed oil, 16
Grape tomatoes, 122
Greek Lamb Kebabs, 6
Greek-style lamb kebabs, 12
Grill grates, oiling, 16
Grilling kebabs, 16–17
Grilling tools, 16
Ground beef
    Gyro Meatball Kebabs with Feta Tzatziki Sauce, 71–72
    Lebanese Beef Kofta, 20
    Meatball Kebab Subs, 23
Ground chuck, 20
Ground lamb, 43
    Gyro Meatball Kebabs wit Feta Tzatziki Sauce, 71–72
    Seekh Kebabs, 67
Ground meats. *See also* Ground beef; Ground lamb
    cooking temperature, 19, 43
    ground pork, 43, 46
    threading kebabs with, 15
Guacamole, Beef Fajita Kebabs with, 32
Gyro Meatball Kebabs with Feta Tzatziki Sauce, 71–72

Halibut, 99, 112
Halloumi cheese, 13, 49, 58, 66, 70, 112, 127
Harissa Beef Kebabs, 30

Hawaiian SPAM and Pineapple Kebabs, 58
Honey-Dijon Salmon Kebabs with Aioli, 110
Horseradish, Citrus-Horseradish Beef Kebabs, 28

Indoor grills, 17

Jalapeño, Mint, and Red Onion Lamb Kebabs, 70
Jamaican Jerk Turkey Kebabs, 96

Kansas City Pork Kebabs, 45
Kasseri cheese, 13, 58, 66, 70
Kebab(s)
    grilling, 16–17
    secrets of the perfect, 8
    serving, 17
Koftas, 8, 10, 15, 20
Korean sesame beef, 37

Lamb. *See also* Ground lamb; Lamb roast
    Greek Lamb Kebabs, 62
    Lamb Shish Kebab, 63
    Pomegranate-Mint Lamb Kebabs, 66
    Seekhh Kebabs, 67
Lamb and Apricot Kebabs (Sosaties), 69
Lamb roast
    Jalapeño, Mint, and Red Onion Lamb Kebabs, 70
    Pomegranate-Mint Lamb Kebabs, 66
    Sosaties (Lamb and Apricot Kebabs), 69
Lamb Shish Kebabs, 63
Lamb shoulder, 43
Lebanese Beef Kofta, 20
Leg of lamb, 43
Lemon-Garlic Baste, 124
Lemon-Garlic Mushroom Kebabs, 124

Lemon-Herb Baste, 93
Lemon-Rosemary Salmon Kebabs, 111

Mahi Mahi Kebabs, Tequila-Lime, 114
Mangoes, 136
Maple-Sage Pork Kebabs, 59
Marinades
    beef kebabs, 19
    Beef Satay, 39
    Buffalo Chicken Wing Kebabs, 82
    Chicken Caesar Salad Kebabs, 90
    Chicken Tikka Kebabs, 77
    Chicken Yakitori, 76
    Citrus-Cilantro, 103
    Citrus-Horseradish Beef Kebabs, 28
    Coconut-Curry, 104
    Cumin-Blood Orange Pork Kebabs, 54
    Egyptian Chicken Kebabs, 78
    Fig and Pork Tenderloin Kebabs, 49
    Filipino Pork Kebabs, 50
    Greek Lamb Kebabs, 62
    Lamb and Apricot Kebabs, 69
    Lamb Shish Kebabs, 63
    Lemon-Rosemary, 111
    Maple-Sage Pork Kebabs, 59
    Pomegranate-Mint Lamb Kebabs, 66
    Pork Pinchos (Spanish Pork Kebabs), 51
    Pork Souvlaki, 44
    Raspberry-Sriracha Glazed Chicken Wing Kebabs, 80–81
    Sambal Shrimp Kebabs, 101
    Sesame Beef Kebabs, 37
    Stir-Fry Vegetable Kebabs, 119
    Sweet Chili, 122
    Tequila-Lime, 114
Mascarapone cheese, 131
Meat(s). *See also* individual types

of meats
    brines for, 12
    grilling vegetables with, 15, 117
    marinating, 12
    properly mixing, 8
    rubs for, 10
    sticking to cooking grate, 16
    threading cubes of, 13–14
    threading strips of, 14–15
Meatball Kebab Subs, 21
Meatballs
    Gyro Meatball Kebabs wit Feta Tzatziki Sauce, 71–72
    Vietnamese Pork Meatballs, 46
Meat thermometer, 14
Metal skewers, 8, 10, 14
Mexican Corn Kebabs, 120
Minced meat kebabs, 8, 15, 16. *See also* Ground meats
Minced meat substitutions, 13
Mint, 62, 66, 70, 72, 78, 106, 132
Mint-Cilantro Pesto, 106
Moroccon-style kebabs, 30
Mushrooms
    Beef Teriyaki Kebabs, 34–35
    Lemon-Garlic Mushroom Kebabs, 124
    Steak and Mushroom Kebabs, 29
    Stir-Fry Vegetable Kebabs, 119
    Summer Vegetable Kebabs, 118
    threading on the skewer, 117
    as vegan/vegetarian alternative, 13
Mustard Barbecue Sauce, 56

Nectarine and Basil Kebabs, 130
Nem Nuong (Vietnamese Pork Meatballs), 46

Oiling grill grates, 16
Onions, 15
    Balsamic-Brown Sugar Steak and Onion Kebabs, 22
    Beef Teriyaki Kebabs, 34–35
    Bratwurst, Onion, and Bell

Pepper Kebabs, 61
Chicken Tikka Kebabs, 77
Cranberry-Hoisin Turkey Kebabs, 95
Cumin-Blood Orange Pork Kebabs, 54
Lamb and Apricot Kebabs, 69
Lamb Shish Kebabs, 63
Stir-Fry Vegetable Kebabs, 119
Summer Vegetable Kebabs, 118
Tandoori Vegetable Kebabs, 125
Vegetable and Halloumi Kebabs, 127
Orange marmalade, 28
Oranges
    Citrus-Cilantro Marinade, 103
    Cumin-Blood Orange Pork Kebabs, 54

Parmesan cheese, 23, 90
Pasilla peppers, 24, 54
Peanut Dipping Sauce, 84–85
Peanut Sauce, Beef Satay with, 38–39
Peppers. *See* Bell peppers
Peruvian Anticuchos, 24
Pineapple/pineapple juice
    Bacon-Wrapped Chicken Kebabs with Pineapple Teriyaki Sauce, 87
    Caribbean Pineapple Kebabs, 135
    Hawaiian SPAM and Pineapple Kebabs, 58
    Rum and Coconut Fruit Kebabs, 136
    Spicy Pineapple Glazed Seafood Kebabs, 109
    Sweet Chili Marinade, 122
    Tequila-Lime Mahi Mahi Kebabs, 114
    Tofu, Tomato, and Sweet Chili Kebabs, 122
Pineapple Teriyaki Sauce, 87
Plum Glaze, 52

Pomegranate-Mint Lamb Kebabs, 66
Pork. *See also* Pork butt; Pork tenderloin
    brines for, 12
    Vietnamese Pork Meatballs, 46
Pork Belly Kebabs with Plum Glaze, 52
Pork butt, 43
    Cumin-Blood Orange Pork Kebabs, 54
    Filipino Pork Kebabs, 50
    Kansas City Pork Kebabs, 45
    Maple-Sage Pork Kebabs, 59
    Pork Kebabs with Mustard BBQ Sauce, 56
    Pork Souvlaki, 44
Pork Kebabs with Mustard BBQ Sauce, 56
Pork Pinchos (Spanish Pork Kebabs), 51
Pork Souvlaki, 44
Pork tenderloin, 43, 51, 55
Portobello mushrooms, 13
Potatoes
    Chicken Sausage and Potato Kebabs, 93
    grilling time, 117
    Steak and Potato Kebabs, 27
Poultry. *See also* Chicken breast; Chicken thighs; Chicken wings; Turkey breast
    best for kebabs, 75
    brines used for, 12
    cooking temperature, 75
Precut "kebab" meat, 14

Raspberry-Sriracha Glazed Chicken Wing Kebabs, 80–81
Roasts, 14, 19. *See also* Chuck roast; Lamb roast; Tri-tip roast
Romain lettuce, Chicken Caesar Salad Kebabs, 89–90
Round roast, 19
Rubs. *See* Spice rubs

Rum, 130, 135, 136
Rum and Coconut Fruit Kebabs, 136
Rump roasts, 19

Salmon filet, 110, 111
Salmon steaks, 99
Sambal Shrimp Kebabs (Sambal Udang), 100–101
Satay, 14, 38–39, 84
Sauces. *See also* Barbecue sauce; Dipping sauces
    Basil Sauce, 130
    Feta Tzatziki Sauce, 72
    Peanut Sauce, 38–39
    Steak Sauce, 36
    Teriyaki Sauce, 35
Scallops, 99, 106, 109
Seafood. *See* Salmon filet; Shrimp
Seekh Kebabs, 8, 10, 15, 67
Seitan, 13
Serving kebabs, 17
Sesame Beef Kebabs, 37
Shish Kebab, Lamb, 63
Shrimp
    Citrus and Cilantro Shrimp Kebabs, 103
    Garlic-Butter Shrimp Kebabs, 102
    grilling, 99
    Sambal Shrimp Kebabs, 100–101
    Spicy Pineapple Glazed Seafood Kebabs, 109
    Thai Cocounut-Curry Shrimp Kebabs, 104
Simple Mint Syrup, 132
Sirloin. *See* Beef sirloin
Skewers
    grilling shrimp using, 99
    for minced and ground meats, 15
    for strips of meat, 15
    types of, 8, 10
Soaking bamboo skewers, 8, 15
Sosaties (Lamb and Apricot Kebabs), 69

Souvlaki, 12
Souvlaki, Pork, 44
SPAM, 58
Spanish Pork Kebabs, 51
Spatulas, 16
Spice rubs, 10
    Bourbon Barbecue Chicken Skewers, 88
    Jamaican Jerk Turkey Kebabs, 96
    Kansas City Pork Kebabs, 45
    Pork Kebabs with Mustard BBQ Sauce, 56
    Spicy Lamb Skewers (Yang Rou Chuan), 64
    Steak and Mushroom Kebabs, 29
    Steakhouse Kebabs, 36
    West African Beef Kebabs, 33
Spicy Lamb Skewers (Yang Rou Chuan), 64
Squash, 15–16, 117
Steak and Mushroom Kebabs, 29
Steak and Potato Kebabs, 27
Steakhouse Kebabs, 36
Steak Sauce, 36
Stir-Fry Vegetable Kebabs, 119
Strips of meat, threading, 14–15
Sub Sandwich, Meatball Kebab, 23
Substitutions, vegan/vegetarian. *See* Vegan/vegetarian substitutes
Summer Vegetable Kebabs, 118
Suya Kebabs, 33
Sweet and Sour Pork Kebabs, 55
Sweet Chili Marinade, 122
Sweet Potato and Browned Butter Kebabs with Feta, 128
Sword skewers, 10
Syrup, Simple Mint Syrup, 132

Tacos
    Carne Asada Kebabs for, 25

Tandoori Vegetable Kebabs, 125
Tempeh, 13
Temperatures
    beef, 19
    for cooking lamb, 43
    for cooking pork, 43
    ground meat, 19
    metal skewers, 16
Tenderloin, 19
Tequila-Lime Mahi Mahi Kebabs, 114
Tequila-Lime Marinade, 114
Teriyaki Kebabs
    beef, 34–35
Teriyaki Sauce, 35, 87
Thai Coconut-Curry Shrimp Kebabs, 104
Thermometer, meat, 14
Threading kebabs, 13–16
    cubes, 13–14
    how to, 13–16
    loosely, 8
    minced/ground meats, 15
    strips, 14–15
    vegetables, 15–16, 117
Tofu, 13, 122
Tofu, Tomato, and Sweet Chili Kebabs, 122
Tomato-Caper Relish, 112
Tomatoes, 111, 112, 122
Tongs, 16
Tortillas, kebabs served in, 25, 32, 41
Tri-tip roast, 19, 25, 27
Tuna, 99
Turkey breast, 75
    Chinese Five Spice Turkey Kebabs, 94
    Cranberry-Hoisin Turkey Kebabs, 95
    Jamaican Jerk Turkey Breast, 96
Tuscan Halibut Kebabs with Tomato-Caper Relish, 112

Vegan/vegetarian substitutes, 13
    beef kebabs, 22, 24, 25, 27, 28, 29, 30, 33, 35, 36, 37, 39, 41
    chicken kebabs, 78, 81. 83, 85, 87, 88, 90, 93, 94, 96
    fish and seafood kebabs, 101, 102, 104, 110, 111, 112
    lamb kebabs, 62, 63, 64, 66, 69, 70
    pork kebabs, 44, 49, 50, 51, 52, 54, 55, 56, 58, 59, 61
Vegetable and Halloumi Kebabs, 127
Vegetables. *See also* specific vegetables
    grilling, 117
    mixing with meat, 15, 117
    mixing with other vegetables, 8
    Summer Vegetable Kebabs, 118
    threading kebabs using, 15–16
Vietnamese Pork Meatballs (Nem Nuong), 46

Watermelon and Simple Mint Syrup Kebabs, 132
West African Beef Kebabs (Suya Kebabs), 33
White mushrooms, 29, 35, 63, 78, 119, 124

Yakitori, 8, 12, 14, 76
Yang Rou Chuan (Spicy Lamb Skewers), 64
Yogurt
    Chicken Kalmi Kebabs, 83
    Chicken Tikka Kebabs, 77
    Egyptian Chicken Kebabs, 78
    Feta Tzatziki Sauce, 72
    Tandoori Vegetable Kebab baste, 125

Zucchini, 117, 118, 119, 125, 127